Principles
in Practice

The Principles in Practice imprint offers teachers concrete illustrations of effective classroom practices based in NCTE research briefs and policy statements. Each book discusses the research on a specific topic, links the research to an NCTE brief or policy statement, and then demonstrates how those principles come alive in practice: by showcasing actual classroom practices that demonstrate the policies in action; by talking about research in practical, teacher-friendly language; and by offering teachers possibilities for rethinking their own practices in light of the ideas presented in the books. Books within the imprint are grouped in strands, each strand focused on a significant topic of interest.

Adolescent Literacy Strand

Adolescent Literacy at Risk? The Impact of Standards (2009) Rebecca Bowers Sipe

Adolescents and Digital Literacies: Learning Alongside Our Students (2010) Sara Kajder

Adolescent Literacy and the Teaching of Reading: Lessons for Teachers of Literature (2010) Deborah Appleman

Rethinking the "Adolescent" in Adolescent Literacy (2017) Sophia Tatiana Sarigianides, Robert Petrone, and Mark A. Lewis

Writing in Today's Classrooms Strand

Writing in the Dialogical Classroom: Students and Teachers Responding to the Texts of Their Lives (2011) Bob Fecho

Becoming Writers in the Elementary Classroom: Visions and Decisions (2011) Katie Van Sluys

Writing Instruction in the Culturally Relevant Classroom (2011) Maisha T. Winn and Latrise P. Johnson

Literacy Assessment Strand

Our Better Judgment: Teacher Leadership for Writing Assessment (2012) Chris W. Gallagher and Eric D. Turley

Beyond Standardized Truth: Improving Teaching and Learning through Inquiry-Based Reading Assessment (2012) Scott Filkins

Reading Assessment: Artful Teachers, Successful Students (2013) Diane Stephens, editor

Literacies of the Disciplines Strand

Entering the Conversations: Practicing Literacy in the Disciplines (2014) Patricia Lambert Stock, Trace Schillinger, and Andrew Stock

Real-World Literacies: Disciplinary Teaching in the High School Classroom (2014) Heather Lattimer

Doing and Making Authentic Literacies (2014) Linda Denstaedt, Laura Jane Roop, and Stephen Best

Reading in Today's Classrooms Strand

Connected Reading: Teaching Adolescent Readers in a Digital World (2015) Kristen Hawley Turner and Troy Hicks

Digital Reading: What's Essential in Grades 3–8 (2015) William L. Bass II and Franki Sibberson

Teaching Reading with YA Literature: Complex Texts, Complex Lives (2016) Jennifer Buehler

Teaching English Language Learners Strand

Beyond "Teaching to the Test": Rethinking Accountability and Assessment for English Language Learners (2017) Betsy Gilliland and Shannon Pella

Community Literacies en Confianza: Learning from Bilingual After-School Programs (2017) Steven Alvarez

Understanding Language: Supporting ELL Students in Responsive ELA Classrooms (2017) Melinda J. McBee Orzulak

Writing across Culture and Language: Inclusive Strategies for Working with ELL Writers in the ELA Classroom (2017) Christina Ortmeier-Hooper

Writing across Culture and Language

Inclusive Strategies for Working with ELL Writers in the ELA Classroom

Christina Ortmeier-Hooper
University of New Hampshire

National Council of Teachers of English
1111 W. Kenyon Road, Urbana, Illinois 61801-1096

Staff Editor: Bonny Graham
Series Editor: Cathy Fleischer
Interior Design: Victoria Pohlmann
Cover Design: Pat Mayer
Cover Image: Marvin Young

NCTE Stock Number: 58531; eStock Number: 58548
ISBN 978-0-8141-5853-1; eISBN 978-0-8141-5854-8

Library of Congress Cataloging-in-Publication Data

Names: Ortmeier-Hooper, Christina 1972- author.
Title: Writing across culture and language : inclusive strategies for working with ELL writers in the ELA classroom / Christina Ortmeier-Hooper.
Description: Urbana, Illinois : National Council of Teachers of English, [2017] I Includes bibliographical references and index. I
Identifiers: LCCN 2017028802 (print) I LCCN 2017048579 (ebook) I ISBN 9780814158548 ( ) I ISBN 9780814158531 (pbk.)
Subjects: LCSH: English language—Study and teaching—Foreign speakers. I English language—Rhetoric—Study and teaching. I English language—Composition and exercises—Study and teaching—Foreign speakers. I Language and culture.
Classification: LCC PE1128.A2 (ebook) I LCC PE1128.A2 0765 2017 (print) I DDC 428.0071/2—dc23
LC record available at https://lccn.loc.gov/2017028802

For Richard (1961–2017) and Andrea, my brother-in-law and sister, two teachers who inspire curiosity and a love of learning in their students. While I was in the final stages of this project, Richard lost his battle with cancer. He was a devoted teacher to his students, and he made me a better person and teacher. This book is dedicated to his memory and to his teaching legacy, which continually reminds so many of us that every student can shine. Rest in peace. You are missed more than you could ever imagine.

Contents

Acknowledgments

I am grateful to the community of teachers, teacher educators, and colleagues who encouraged me throughout this project. Thank you to Tom Newkirk, Alecia Magnifico, Cris Beemer, Marcos Del Hierro, Soo Hyon Kim, Liz Kirwan, Laura Smith, Tina Proulx, Gail Fensom, Katherine Earley, Kristen Raymond, Kerry Enright, Judy Sharkey, and many others who nudged me forward and helped me refine ideas and words. I would like to thank my home institution, the University of New Hampshire, which granted me a sabbatical at an important juncture with this project, giving me the time to bring this book to completion. I am also grateful to the wonderful editors and staff at the National Council of Teachers of English, which has been a professional home for me since I began teaching in the 1990s. In particular, I am grateful to my editor, Cathy Fleischer, who shared her vision for this series when it was just beginning and then invited me to write this book. Throughout this process, Cathy has proved to be a compassionate editor and reader, encouraging me and offering sage advice as each chapter unfolded. She helped me to find my voice, to forge forward, and to think deeply about the literacy practices of multilingual students and the concerns of their teachers. Her patience, kindness, and insights have helped me bring these ideas and pages together. I am also grateful to NCTE's Bonny Graham, senior editor, for her guidance during the final stages of this process.

My family has made all of this possible. I am thankful to my husband, Tom, for his support, his willingness to listen to drafts, and the many meals that he made happen while this project was underway. I also want to thank my wonderful sons—Johnathan, Sean, and Zachary—for their encouragement, their help in collating various draft pages, their patience as Mom wrote and researched, and their love. They continually inspire me with their own interests, their perseverance, and their kindness toward others.

Finally, I'd like to thank the students, those featured in this book and those in classrooms I have taught in the past. They continue to inspire my work, research, and advocacy as they strive each day to further their own education and futures.

NCTE Position Paper on the Role of English Teachers in Educating English Language Learners (ELLs)

Prepared by the NCTE ELL Task Force
Approved by the NCTE Executive Committee, April 2006

This position paper is designed to address the knowledge and skills mainstream teachers need to have in order to develop effective curricula that engage English language learners, develop their academic skills, and help them negotiate their identities as bilingual learners. More specifically, this paper addresses the language and literacy needs of these learners as they participate and learn in English-medium classes. NCTE has made clear bilingual students' right to maintain their native languages (see "On Affirming the CCCC 'Students' Right to Their Own Language'" 2003). Thus, this paper addresses ways teachers can help these students develop English as well as ways they can support their students' bilingualism. In the United States bilingual learners, more commonly referred to as English language learners, are defined as students who know a language other than English and are learning English. Students' abilities range from being non-English speakers to being fully proficient. The recommendations in this paper apply to all of them.

Context

The National Clearinghouse for English Language Acquisition (NCELA) reported that in 2003–04 there were over five million English language learners (ELLs) in schools in the United States (NCELA, 2004). In the last ten years the ELL population has grown 65%, and the diversity of those students continues to challenge teachers and schools. Although 82% of ELLs in the United States are native Spanish speakers, Hopstock and Stephenson (2003) found that school districts identified over 350 different first languages for their second language learners.

Federal, state, and local policies have addressed the education of bilingual learners by implementing different types of programs. Different models of bilingual education, English as a Second Language, English immersion, and integration into mainstream classes, sometimes referred to as submersion, are among the most common approaches. Preferences for the types of programs have changed over time, responding to demographic and political pressures. (For a historical and descriptive summary, see NCTE's "Position Statement on Issues in ESL and Bilingual Education"; Brisk, 2006; Crawford, 2004.)

The best way to educate bilingual learners has been at the center of much controversy. Research points to the advantage of quality bilingual programs (Greene, 1997; Ramirez, 1992; Rolstad, Mahoney, & Glass, 2005; Thomas & Collier, 2002; Willig, 1985) and the benefits of ESL instruction when language is taught through content (Freeman, Y. S., & Freeman, D. E., 1998; Marcia, 2000).

The Role of English Teachers in Educating ELLs

For a variety of reasons, however, the majority of ELLs find themselves in mainstream classrooms taught by teachers with little or no formal professional development in teaching such students (Barron & Menken, 2002; Kindler, 2002). Although improving the education of ELLs has been proposed as a pressing national educational priority (Waxman & Téllez, 2002), many teachers are not adequately prepared to work with a linguistically diverse student population (American Federation of Teachers, 2004; Fillmore & Snow, 2002; Gándara, Rumberger, Maxwell-Jolly, & Callahan, 2003; Menken & Antunez, 2001; Nieto, 2003).

Teachers working to better meet the needs of linguistically diverse students need support. NCTE encourages English teachers to collaborate and work closely with ESL and bilingual teaching professionals, who can offer classroom support, instructional advice, and general insights into second language acquisition. School administrators should support and encourage teachers to attend workshops and professional conferences that regularly offer sessions on bilingual learners, particularly in the areas of reading and writing. Schools should also consider seeking professional development for their teachers from neighboring colleges.

In turn, colleges and universities providing teacher education should offer all preservice teachers, as well as teachers pursuing advanced degree work, preparation in teaching linguistically diverse learners in their future classrooms. Coursework should be offered on second language writing and reading, and on second language acquisition, as well as on culture, and should be encouraged for all teachers.

Who Are the Students?

Bilingual students differ in various ways, including level of oral English proficiency, literacy ability in both the heritage language and English, and cultural backgrounds. English language learners born in the United States often develop conversational language abilities in English but lack academic language proficiency. Newcomers, on the other hand, need to develop both conversational and academic English. Education previous to entering U.S. schools helps determine students' literacy levels in their native language. Some learners may have age-/grade-level skills, while others have limited or no literacy because of the quality of previous schooling, interrupted schooling due to wars or migration, and other circumstances (Suárez-Orozco & Suárez-Orozco, 2001). Given the wide range of English language learners and their backgrounds, it is important that all teachers take the time to learn about their students, particularly in terms of their literacy histories.

Immigrant students and the children of immigrants in the United States come from many cultural backgrounds. The background knowledge English learners bring to school greatly affects their performance. For this reason, teachers of English language learners should be sure to build background for content lessons rather than assuming that bilingual students come with the same background knowledge as mainstream students.

Teaching Bilingual Learners in Mainstream Classrooms

This section specifically addresses teaching language, reading, and writing, as well as the specific kinds of academic literacy that are often a part of most English and language arts curricula. Although English language arts teachers have literacy as the focus of their teaching, many of these suggestions are useful for teachers working in the content areas as well. To acquire academic content through English, English language learners need to learn English. The academic language that students need in the different content areas differs, and students need scaffolding to help them to learn both the English language and the necessary content. For English language learners, teachers need to consider content objectives as well as English language development objectives.

Bilinguals need three types of knowledge to become literate in a second language. They need to know the second language; they need to know literacy; and they need world knowledge (Bernhardt, 1991). The sections below list key ideas for helping English language learners develop academic English proficiency. More detailed information on the topics covered in this section can be obtained from the topical bibliography compiled as part of this project.

To teach bilingual learners, teachers must get to know their learners.

Knowledge of the Students

Knowledge of the students is key to good teaching. Because teachers relate to students both as learners and as children or adolescents, teachers must establish how they will address these two types of relationships, what they need to know about their students, and how they will acquire this knowledge. The teacher-learner relationship implies involvement between teachers and students around subject matter and language and literacy proficiency in both languages. Adult-child relationships are more personal and should include the family. Focusing on both types of relationships bridges the gap between school and the world outside it, a gap that is especially important for many bilingual students whose world differs greatly from school.

Teaching Language

Second language learners need to develop academic proficiency in English to master content-area subjects. Teachers can provide effective instruction for these students by:

- Recognizing that second language acquisition is a gradual developmental process and is built on students' knowledge and skill in their native language;
- Providing authentic opportunities to use language in a nonthreatening environment;
- Teaching key vocabulary connected with the topic of the lesson;
- Teaching academic oral language in the context of various content areas;
- Teaching text- and sentence-level grammar in context to help students understand the structure and style of the English language;
- Teaching the specific features of language students need to communicate in social as well as academic contexts.

The Role of English Teachers in Educating ELLs

Teaching Literacy: Reading

Bilingual students also need to learn to read and write effectively in order to succeed in school.

Teachers can support English language learners' literacy development by:

- Introducing classroom reading materials that are culturally relevant;
- Connecting the readings with the students' background knowledge and experiences;
- Encouraging students to discuss the readings, including the cultural dimensions of the text;
- Having students read a more accessible text on the topic before reading the assigned text;
- Asking families to read with students a version in the heritage language;
- Replacing discrete skill exercises and drills with many opportunities to read;
- Providing opportunities for silent reading in either the students' first language or in English;
- Reading aloud frequently to allow students to become familiar with and appreciate the sounds and structures of written language;
- Reading aloud while students have access to the text to facilitate connecting oral and written modalities;
- Stimulating students' content knowledge of the text before introducing the text;
- Teaching language features, such as text structure, vocabulary, and text- and sentence-level grammar to facilitate comprehension of the text;
- Recognizing that first and second language growth increases with abundant reading and writing.

Support reading comprehension by:

- Relating the topic to the cultural experiences of the students;
- "Front loading" comprehension via a walk through the text or a preview of the main ideas, and other strategies that prepare students for the topic of the text;
- Having students read a more accessible text on the topic before reading the assigned text;
- Asking families to read with students a version in the heritage language;
- Doing pre-reading activities that elicit discussion of the topic;
- Teaching key vocabulary essential for the topic;
- Recognizing that experiences in writing can be used to clarify understanding of reading.

Teaching Literacy: Writing

Writing well in English is often the most difficult skill for English language learners to master. Many English language learners are still acquiring vocabulary and syntactic competence in their writing. Students may show varying degrees of acquisition, and not all second language writers will have the same difficulties or challenges. Teachers should be aware

The Role of English Teachers in Educating ELLs

that English language learners may not be familiar with terminology and routines often associated with writing instruction in the United States, including writing process, drafting, revision, editing, workshop, conference, audience, purpose, or genre. Furthermore, certain elements of discourse, particularly in terms of audience and persuasion, may differ across cultural contexts. The same is true for textual borrowing and plagiarism. The CCCC Statement on Second Language Writing and Writers is a useful resource for all teachers of writing to examine.

Teachers can provide instructional support for English language learners in their writing by:

- Providing a nurturing environment for writing;
- Introducing cooperative, collaborative writing activities which promote discussion;
- Encouraging contributions from all students, and promoting peer interaction to support learning;
- Replacing drills and single-response exercises with time for writing practice;
- Providing frequent meaningful opportunities for students to generate their own texts;
- Designing writing assignments for a variety of audiences, purposes, and genres, and scaffolding the writing instruction;
- Providing models of well-organized papers for the class. Teachers should consider glossing sample papers with comments that point to the specific aspects of the paper that make it well written;
- Offering comments on the strength of the paper, in order to indicate areas where the student is meeting expectations;
- Making comments explicit and clear (both in written response and in oral responses). Teachers should consider beginning feedback with global comments (content and ideas, organization, thesis) and then move on to more local concerns (or mechanical errors) when student writers are more confident with the content of their draft;
- Giving more than one suggestion for change—so that students still maintain control of their writing;
- Not assuming that every learner understands how to cite sources or what plagiarism is. Teachers should consider talking openly about citation and plagiarism in class, exploring the cultural values that are implicit in the rules of plagiarism and textual borrowing, and noting that not all cultures ascribe to the same rules and guidelines. Students should be provided with strategies for avoiding plagiarism.

Teaching Language and Content

The best way to help students learn both English and the knowledge of school subjects is to teach language through content. This should not replace reading and writing instruction in English, nor study of literature and grammar. There are three key reasons to do this:

1. **Students get both language and content.**
   Research has shown that students can learn English and subject matter content material

at the same time. Students don't need to delay the study of science or literature until they reach high levels of English. Instead, they can learn both simultaneously. Given the time limitations older students face, it is crucial that classes provide them with both academic content-area knowledge and academic English.

2. **Language is kept in its natural context.**
When teachers teach science in English, students learn science terms as they study biology or chemistry. The vocabulary occurs naturally as students read and discuss science texts.

3. **Students have reasons to use language for real purposes.**
The primary purpose of school is to help students develop the knowledge of different academic disciplines. When academic content is presented in English, students focus on the main purpose of schooling: learning science, math, social studies, or literature. In the process, they also learn English.

Selecting Materials

- Choose a variety of texts around a theme.
- Choose texts at different levels of difficulty.
- Choose reading and writing materials that represent the cultures of the students in the class.
- When possible, include texts in the native languages of the ELLs in the class. The following considerations should be used as a guide for choosing texts that support bilingual learners:
    - Materials should include both literature and informational texts.
    - Materials should include culturally relevant texts.
    - Authentic materials should be written to inform or entertain, not to teach a grammar point or a letter-sound correspondence.
    - The language of the text should be natural.
    - If translated, the translation should be good language.
    - Materials should include predictable text for emergent readers.
    - Materials should include texts with nonlinguistic cues that support comprehension (For a more comprehensive checklist, see Freeman, Y. S., & Freeman, D. E., 2002; Freeman, D. E., & Freeman, Y. S., 2004.)

Low-Level Literacy Immigrant Students

Late-arrival immigrant and refugee students with low literacy skills have been found to benefit from Newcomer programs or Welcome Centers designed for 1–3 semesters of high school (Boyson & Short, 2003; Schnur, 1999; Short, 2002). The focus is to help students acquire beginning English skills and guide students' acculturation to the U.S. school system before enrollment in regular ESL language support programs or content-area classrooms. The integration of such programs in high school English departments should be encouraged.

Conclusion

As the number of bilingual learners in mainstream classes increases, it becomes even more important for mainstream teachers to use effective practices to engage these students so that they can acquire the academic English and the content-area knowledge they need for school success. The guidelines offered here are designed as initial suggestions for teachers to follow. However, we recognize that all teachers need much more. Teachers need continued support and professional development to enable all their students, including their bilingual students, to succeed.

References

American Federation of Teachers. (March, 2004). *Closing the achievement gap: Focus on Latino students* (Policy Brief 17). Retrieved March 28, 2006, from http://www.aft.org/teachers/pusbs-reports/index.htm#english.

Barron, V., & Menken, K. (2002). *What are the characteristics of the bilingual education and ESL teacher shortage?* Washington, D.C.: National Clearinghouse for English Language Acquisition and Language Instruction Educational Programs.

Bernhardt, E. B. (1991). A psycholinguistic perspective on second language literacy. Reading in Two Languages. *AILA Review, 8*, 31–44.

Boyson, B. A., & Short, D. J. (2003). *Secondary school newcomer programs in the United States* (Research Report 12). Santa Cruz, CA, and Washington, DC: Center for Research on Education Diversity & Excellence.

Brisk, M. E. (2006). *Bilingual education: From compensatory to quality schooling.* (2nd ed.) Mahwah, NJ: Erlbaum.

Crawford, J. (2004). *Educating English learners.* Los Angeles: Bilingual Education Services.

De Jong, E. J. (2002). Effective bilingual education: From theory to academic achievement in a two-way bilingual program. *Bilingual Research Journal, 26*(1), 1–15.

Fillmore, L. W., & Snow, C. (2002). What teachers need to know about language. In C. T. Adger, C. Snow, & D. Christian (Eds.), *What teachers need to know about language* (pp. 7–53). Washington, DC: Center for Applied Linguistics.

Freeman, D. E., and Freeman, Y. S. (2004). *Essential linguistics: What you need to know to teach reading, ESL, spelling, phonics, and grammar.* Portsmouth, NH: Heinemann.

Freeman, Y. S., & Freeman, D. E. (1998). *ESL/EFL teaching: Principles for success.* Portsmouth, NH: Heinemann.

Freeman, Y. S., and Freeman, D. E. (2002). *Closing the achievement gap.* Portsmouth, NH: Heinemann.

Gándara, P., Rumberger, R., Maxwell-Jolly, J., & Callahan, R. (2003). English learners in California schools: Unequal resources, unequal outcomes. *Education Policy Analysis Archives, 11*(36). Retrieved March 28, 2006, from http://epaa.asu.edu/.

Gibbons, P. (2002). *Scaffolding language, scaffolding learning: Teaching second language learners in the mainstream classroom.* Portsmouth, NH: Heinemann.

Greene, J. P. (1997). A meta-analysis of the Rossell and Baker review of bilingual education research. *Bilingual Research Journal, 21.*

The Role of English Teachers in Educating ELLs

Hopstock, P. & Stephenson, T. (2003). *Native languages of limited English proficient students.* U.S. Department of Education. Retrieved March 5, 2006.

Kindler, A. L. (2002). *Survey of the states' limited English proficient students and available educational programs and services 1999–2000 summary report.* Washington, DC: National Clearinghouse for English Language Acquisition and Language Instruction Education Programs (NCELA). Retrieved Dec. 26, 2003, from http://www.ncela.gwu.edu.

Krashen, S. (1996). *Under attack: The case against bilingual education.* Culver City, CA: Language Education Associates.

McQuillan, J., & Tse, L. (1997). Does research matter? An analysis of media opinion of bilingual education, 1984–1994. *Bilingual Research Journal, 20*(1), 1–27.

Menken, K., & Antunez, B. (2001). *An overview of the preparation and certification of teachers working with limited English proficient students.* Washington, DC: National Clearinghouse of Bilingual Education. Retrieved July 28, 2003, from http://www.ericsp.org/pages/digests/ncbe.pdf.

NCELA. (2006). *The growing number of limited English proficient students 1991–2002.* Washington, DC: U.S. Department of Education.

Nieto, S. M. (2003). *What keeps teachers going?* New York: Teachers College.

Pally, M. (Ed.) (2000). *Sustained content teaching in academic ESL/EFL: A practical approach.* Boston: Houghton Mifflin.

Ramirez, J. D. (1992). Executive summary. *Bilingual Research Journal, 16,* 1–62.

Rolstad, K., Mahoney, K., & Glass, G. V. (2005) The big picture: A meta-analysis of program effectiveness research on English language learners. *Educational Policy, 19,* 572–594.

Schnur, B. (1999). A newcomer's high school. *Educational Leadership, 56*(7), 50–52.

Short, D. J. (2002). Newcomer programs: An educational alternative for secondary immigrant students. *Education and Urban Society, 34*(2), 173–198.

Solomon, J., & Rhodes, N. (1995). *Conceptualizing academic language.* Washington, DC: The National Center for Research on Cultural Diversity and Second Language Learning.

Suárez-Orozco, C., & Suárez-Orozco, M. M. (2001). *Children of immigration.* Cambridge, MA: Harvard University.

Thomas, W. P., & Collier, V. P. (2002). *A national study of school effectiveness for language minority students' long-term academic achievement.* Santa Cruz, CA: Center for Research on Education, Diversity & Excellence, University of California, Santa Cruz.

Waxman, H. C., & Téllez, K. (2002). *Research synthesis on effective teaching practices for English language learners* (Publication Series No. 3). Philadelphia: Mid-Atlantic Regional Educational Laboratory.

Willig, A. C. (1985). A meta-analysis of selected studies on the effectiveness of bilingual education. *Review of Educational Research, 55*(3), 269–317.

For more resources to support English language learners, see http://www.ncte.org/positions/statements/teacherseducatingell.

Statement of Terminology and Glossary

Steven Alvarez, St. John's University
Betsy Gilliland, University of Hawai`i Mānoa
Christina Ortmeier-Hooper, University of New Hampshire
Melinda J. McBee Orzulak, Bradley University
Shannon Pella, California State University, Sacramento

As authors of the various books in the Teaching English Language Learners strand of the NCTE Principles in Practice (PIP) imprint, we have made a concerted effort to use consistent terminology in these volumes. All of us have thought long and hard about the ways in which we label and describe bilingual and ELL students and the programs that often provide these students with additional support. Even so, readers will notice some variation in terms used to describe students, classrooms, and teaching practices. The concern over terminology is part of a long-standing discussion and trends in the labeling of these students, as well as of the fields that conduct research on teachers and students working across languages to teach and learn English. Often the shifting among terms leads to confusion and contention for teachers, administrators, teacher educators, and policymakers.

To address this confusion and tension, we begin each book in this strand with a glossary of common terms and acronyms that are part of current discussions about meeting the needs of these students in English language arts classrooms and beyond. For many readers, the terms themselves and the ongoing shift to new terms can be alienating, the jargon dividing readers into insiders and outsiders. But often the shift in terms has a great deal to do with both policy and issues of identity for students. For example, up until the No Child Left Behind (NCLB) Act of 2001, most educational documents referred to these students as *bilingual* or *ESL*, both of which acknowledge that English is a second language and that a student has a first language as well.

The term *English language learner* was adopted with NCLB and brought into our schools and the larger public discourse. In fact, in 2002 the US Department of Education renamed the Office of Bilingual Education and Minority Languages Affairs. It became the Office of English Language Acquisition, Language Enhancement and Academic Achievement for Limited English Proficient Students, now identified simply as the Office of English Language Acquisition (OELA). The change indicated a shift away from acknowledging students' home languages or bilingual abilities. Close to two decades later, the term *English language learner* remains prominent in educational policy and in many textbooks geared toward teachers and teacher educators. Its prominence and familiarity in the literature makes it an accessible way to talk about these students. Yet, as we have heard from many students through the years, the term *English language learner* can also be limiting. As one student asked, "When do I stop being an English language learner and get to just be an English language user?" The term also works against efforts to acknowledge the competencies and linguistically sophisticated talents these students have as translators, bilingual speakers, and cross-cultural negotiators.

Statement of Terminology and Glossary

In these PIP volumes, we use the term *English language learner* as a way to reach out to readers who see and hear this term regularly used in their schools, in their hallways, and in other helpful books in the field. However, some of us also use the terms *multilingual* or *bilingual* in order to encourage a discussion of these young people not simply as novice English learners but as individuals with linguistic and academic competencies they have gained from bilingual/multilingual experiences and literacies.

Glossary

Bilingual, multilingual, or plurilingual: These terms refer to the ability to use (i.e., speak, write, and/or read) multiple languages. For many ELL-designated students in US schools, English is actually the third or fourth language they have learned, making *bilingual* not necessarily an accurate term.

Emergent bilingual: This term has been proposed as a more appropriate term than *LEP* or *ELL*, because it points to possibilities of developing bilingualism rather than focusing on language limits or deficiencies (García, 2009).

English as a foreign language (EFL): Refers to non-native English-speaking students who are learning English in a country where English is not the primary language.

English as an international language (EIL) or English as a lingua franca (ELF): These are terms used to refer to global conceptions of English, or English used for communication between members of various nations.

English as a second language (ESL): Readers may be most familiar with this term because it has been used as an overarching term for students, programs, and/or a field of study. Currently the term usually refers to programs of instruction (i.e., study of English in an English-speaking country); however, *ESL* was used in the past to refer to English language learning students.

English language learner (ELL): In keeping with the terminology used in the *NCTE Position Paper on the Role of English Teachers in Educating English Language Learners (ELLs)*, this PIP strand employs the term *ELL*, which is commonly used in secondary schools as the short form of *English language learner*. The term refers to a complex, heterogeneous range of students who are in the process of learning English.

English learner (EL): This is the preferred term of the California Department of Education (and, increasingly, other states). California is the state with the largest number and percentage of emergent bilingual students enrolled in public schools. Over the past twenty years, California has moved from *LEP* to *ELL* and, most recently, from *ELL* to *EL*.

First language (L1) and second language (L2): *L1* has been used to refer to students' "mother tongue" or "home language" as they learn additional languages (referred to as *L2*).

Generation 1.5: This term, originally used in higher education, often refers to students who have been long-term residents in the United States but who were born abroad (al-

Statement of Terminology and Glossary

though the term is sometimes also used to refer to US-born children of recent immigrants). The designation of 1.5 describes their feelings of being culturally between first- and second-generation immigrants; they are often fluent in spoken English but may still be working to command aspects of written English, especially academic writing. As long-term residents, these students may reject *ESL* as a term that has been used to refer to recent immigrants to the United States.

Limited English proficiency (LEP): This abbreviation may be used in some educational contexts to refer to a designation used by the US Department of Education. Many scholars see this as a deficit term because of its focus on subtractive language (language that implies a deficiency) under a monolingual assumption of proficiency.

Long-term English language learner (LTELL): Currently in use in some states, this term refers to K–12 students who have been enrolled in US schools for many years and continue to be stuck with the ELL designation long past the time it should take for redesignation. Like Generation 1.5 students, LTELLs may have spent most if not all of their education in US schools. For a variety of reasons, including family mobility, inconsistent educational programs, and personal reasons, they have not had opportunities to learn academic language sufficiently to pass English language proficiency tests and other measures of proficiency for redesignation (Olsen, 2010).

Mainstream: This term is increasingly antiquated due to shifting demographics in the United States. In practice, it often refers to nonremedial, nonhonors, nonsheltered classes and programs. Sometimes it is used to refer to native or monolingual English speakers as a norm; changing demographics, however, mean that schools increasingly have a majority of culturally and linguistically diverse students, so it's been argued that a linguistically diverse classroom is the "New Mainstream" (Enright, 2011).

Monolingual: This term is used to refer to people who speak only one language, although often this label masks speakers' fluent use of multiple dialects, or variations, of English—an issue of particular concern when working with culturally diverse students who use other varieties of English (such as Hawai'i Pidgin or African American Vernacular) in their lives outside of school. The monolingual English label can mask these diverse students' need to learn academic English just as much as their immigrant classmates do. Much of what this PIP strand discusses is relevant to students who utilize multiple varieties of English; teachers can support these students by acknowledging their multilingualism and helping them learn to use English for academic and other purposes.

Native or non-native English speakers (NES, NNES): Some materials contrast native English speakers (NES) with non-native English speakers (NNES). As with *monolingual*, the term *native speaker* is increasingly unclear, given how many long-term ELLs speak English fluently without a "foreign" accent and yet technically have another world language as their home or first language.

Newcomer: Some school districts have separate one-year programs for "newcomers," or students who are newly arrived in the United States, in which students learn not just "surviv-

Statement of Terminology and Glossary

al" English, but also how school works in the United States. As the position statement discusses, it's sometimes argued that newcomer programs benefit "low-level literacy immigrant students" and/or students with interrupted formal education who may have limited literacy in their first language (L1). Other newcomers may be fully literate in L1, especially by high school, and may or may not benefit from being isolated from the mainstream curriculum. For older students, the challenge is to move away from "low-level" ideas of literacy assessment that may discount the literacies of these students.

Resident or local bilingual, multilingual, or plurilingual: These terms are sometimes used to refer to students who reside in the United States (in contrast to those who are on student visas). Resident students may or may not be US citizens, others may not have permanent resident status, while still others may not have immigration documentation at all.

References

Enright, K. A. (2011). Language and literacy for a new mainstream. *American Educational Research Journal, 48*(1), 80–118. doi:10.3102/0002831210368989

García, O. (2009). Emergent bilinguals and TESOL: What's in a name? *TESOL Quarterly, 43*(2), 322–26. doi:10.1002/j.1545-7249.2009.tb00172.x

Olsen, L. (2010). *Reparable harm: Fulfilling the unkept promise of educational opportunity for California's long term English learners.* Long Beach, CA: Californians Together.

Chapter One

How *Do* ELL Students Write across Language and Culture?

Down the Hall

It is Monday morning, and the students have streamed into the classroom. On the walls are world maps and pictures of flags from various countries: Iraq, Haiti, Dominican Republic, Somalia, Mexico, Guatemala, China, Nepal. The desks are placed in rows, each one numbered. Some students talk in the doorway, then slowly move toward their desks. The melodies of Haitian Creole, Spanish, Nepalese, and Arabic echo from the hallways into the classroom as the students move into their seats. In the front row, a lone young student from China pulls out a handheld translator. At the front of the classroom is a podium, a whiteboard, and a bulletin board filled with vocabulary—a word wall built by teacher and students featuring academic language and terms from social studies, science classrooms, and English language arts (ELA) classrooms. Though this is an English as a second language (ESL) classroom, each of these students has an ELA teacher down the hall, and each one will take ELA classes throughout his or her high school career.

Each of the students attends class in this room once a day. Some may have additional support in a study hall with an aide or teacher specializing in teaching English language learners (ELLs) who can help them navigate their homework in the content areas. The ELL teacher would tell you that many people tend to place all language learners into a single box or profile, to describe them in terms of "limited English proficiency" (LEP), or question how English proficiency impedes their learning. But she knows there are vast differences and experiences among these students. She is careful to look for the surprises and the literacy strengths, to not judge prematurely—especially during a newcomer's silent period. She is always searching for clues into their literacy pasts and their current language experiences in order to build on past knowledge and out-of-school literacies. Many of these ELL students become more adept at English reading and writing over time, and they will test out of ELL support. Some will continue to struggle for years to pass the English writing proficiency exam. Almost all of them will continue to need support in writing to one degree or another because it's the most difficult language skill to master.

In this school, the ELA teacher and the ESL teacher seldom cross paths, despite the fact that they share similar teaching objectives around reading, writing, and language development. Common planning periods are rare, and those that exist are often taken up by other activities and priorities. Teachers here know that they share the same students, and often engage in brief check-ins during hallway duty to see how one student or another is fairing in the mainstream ELA classroom. Quick tips and insights during these moments happen quite often, but sustained conversations on teaching writing to ELLs and multilinguals is not the norm.

I know this reality well. I began my teaching career as a certified high school ELA and ELL teacher, wearing both hats over the course of the day. My first teaching experiences were as an ELA teacher in a summer program for students labeled "at-risk" in an urban US school district. I went on to teach high school ELA and ELL, spending half my day with juniors in classes on composition, American literature, and poetry and the other half working with ELL students down the hall. I then became a full-time ELL teacher specializing in language arts, reading, and writing. I developed curricula for my ELLs that aimed to dovetail with ELA standards. As a teacher of writing, I was fortunate to learn my craft from Tom Romano, Thomas Newkirk, and Don Graves, and through reading the works of Nancie Atwell, George Hillocks, and Linda Rief. My English for Speakers of Other Languages (ESOL) training had also been rich, filled with the works of bilingual educators such as Guadalupe Valdés, Yvonne Freeman, and Carole Edelsky. But I'll be honest. When I began teaching, there was very little information about how to work with ELL students specifically on writing. Though I was fortunate to take a methods course dedicated to the teaching of writing in ELA courses, the coursework and readings did not prepare me for the obstacles that my ELL students would face when it came to writing. Likewise, when I started teaching, Teachers of English to Speakers of Other Languages (TESOL) courses in curriculum, instruction, and assessment often relegated writing to the last of the four language skills; reading, listening, and speaking took precedence, along with teaching vocabulary and grammar.

A great deal has changed since I began teaching, from the No Child Left Behind Act (2001) and the Every Student Succeeds Act (2015) to the adoption of the Common Core State Standards (CCSS) and other state-designed internal standards closely aligned to the Common Core State Standards Initiative (2010). In addition, a recognized field of second language writing emerged in the 1990s. Today, we have research and academic journals focused solely on multilingual writers and writing, though most of these continue to look almost exclusively at university-level students or students studying English in foreign countries. Still, today in the United States, we have some teacher education programs offering courses and workshops on teaching multilingual writers; others make TESOL coursework a part of degree and licensure requirements. These changes are part of more general interest in student writing and the teaching of writing in our schools—for all students in general and for multilingual students in particular. In part, the interest in writing is one element of a larger educational and economic trend. Over the past two decades, we have seen writing expand in terms of its stature in the curriculum, its place in educational assessments, and its currency within the workplace.

The Purpose of This Book

Today, there are approximately 4.6 million English language learners in US schools, and that number is expected to rise over the next decade (National Center for Education Statistics, 2017). By 2025, it is estimated that more than 25 percent of public school students will be English language learners or multilinguals (US Department of Education, 2006). We know that ELA teachers will serve as the primary writing teacher for many of these students at one point or another during their secondary school years. We also realize that writing well is a threshold skill—for all students (National Commission on Writing, 2004; Applebee & Langer, 2011). The ability to write well can open doors for students; it creates opportunities in the workplace, can determine entrance into higher education and scholarship programs, and can even determine access within a given high school's upper-level academic tracks.

This book aims to provide examples and research-based practices for ELA teachers working with ELL and multilingual writers. It is aligned with specific writing instruction recommendations outlined in the *NCTE Position Paper on the Role of English Teachers in Educating English Language Learners (ELLs)*. Specifically, the book develops concrete understandings and strategies for teachers on the following concepts detailed in the *Position Paper*'s "Teaching Literacy: Writing" section (the Position Paper is reprinted in the front matter of this book):

- Second language students have varying degrees of language acquisition and writing backgrounds. Certain elements of discourse, conventions of a genre, and writing expectations vary across cultural contexts.

- To generate their own texts, ELL and multilingual students need rich instruction and meaningful writing opportunities (e.g., teachers can provide scaffolded and inquiry-based writing instruction; replace single-response exercises with time for meaningful writing practice; and design inclusive and varied writing assignments).

- Teachers should foster meaningful interactions and discussions around writing for ELLs (e.g., introducing cooperative, collaborative writing activities that promote discussion; encouraging contributions from all students; and encouraging peer interaction to support learning).

- ELL writers require explicit and clear teacher response, benchmarks and modeling, and more attentive systems of feedback (e.g., teachers can develop new strategies for using models of well-organized papers in class; refine techniques for responding to ELLs' texts; develop best practices for error correction; and create classroom practices that build confidence and competency in ELL writers).

- Late-arrival immigrants and refugees with low-literacy and/or interrupted schooling may have specific challenges that require additional strategies and support.

To meet these goals, I draw on theory, research, and practical applications from the fields of TESOL and second language writing. The book highlights connections between theory and classroom application, with particular attention to classroom implementation and learners' experiences. Since adolescent ELL writers' perspectives can remain hidden from their ELA teachers, this book also draws attention to students' experiences and perspectives. I recognize that struggles with English writing often mask the communicative strengths of many intelligent, bright, linguistically and culturally diverse students; this, in turn, hinders them from achieving higher levels of academic advancement. For these reasons, this book challenges deficit models of ELL writers and offers techniques that help teachers identify their students' strengths and develop inclusive research-based writing practices that are helpful to all student writers.

Why Focus on Writing?

Writing well acts as a gate-opener (and gatekeeper) to the major access points for students aiming to do well in secondary schools and beyond. Teachers, guidance counselors, and administrators use student writing samples and tests to determine which students are invited into honors, AP, and other upper-level academic tracks. Writing résumés and professional materials such as workplace correspondence, cover letters, and job applications opens doors to employment. College and scholarship applications ask students to write essays that help determine college acceptance, merit, and financial need. Students' essays help determine which colleges accept students, which majors they can enter, and how much money in aid a student may receive (Wight, 2017). Once college is completed, writing continues to be important; employers report that writing matters in the workplace. In discussions of hiring and promotion trends, employers note that those who write well tend to move up more quickly, have higher salaries, gain leadership roles, and in general receive more opportunities (National Commission on Writing, 2004). Quite simply, writing well is a way of opening doors and gaining access to a number of financial, professional, personal, and academic opportunities.

For thousands of ELL and multilingual students, however, writing closes doors. Research tells us that for these students, writing will be the greatest area of struggle and lack of confidence (Chiang & Schmida, 2006; Ortmeier-Hooper, 2013; Kanno & Kangas, 2014; Ruecker, 2015). Research also has shown that writing well *in a second language* is the most difficult cognitive and language skill for multilingual and ELL students to master (Harklau, 1994). I emphasize "in a second language" because the process, cognitive demands, and identity issues inherent in writing in a second language are unique and very different from writing in one's first language (Silva, 1993).

Writing in a Second Language (L2) or Even Third Language (L3)

What Have Been Your Own Experiences with Writing in a Foreign Language?

In workshops across the country, I often ask teachers to respond to a prompt that asks them to write in a language other than English. Over the seven minutes of writing time, they begin to understand—on visceral, intellectual, and emotional levels—the kinds of challenges their ELL students face. As they reflect on the experience, teachers say the following:

- "I stopped writing. I resented feeling like I couldn't express myself."
- "I switched topics—I couldn't write in response to the prompt you gave. I didn't have the vocabulary, so I wrote about the weather, my cat, etc."

- "I kept crossing things out. I struggled to get the verb tense right. I knew it was wrong, and I just couldn't keep writing. I felt like I was constantly stopping and starting. I felt like I was always interrupting myself. I only wrote two sentences."

- "I gave up."

- "I started writing in French, but then I started using English words to fill in the blanks, the words that I couldn't remember. I kept confusing word order, too."

- "What I wrote is so much shorter than what I usually can write. I just felt so silenced. Every word seems to take so long to get on paper."

- "I never started. I took French for four years, and I have no idea or confidence in writing it. It felt impossible. I kept looking around at other people's papers. Everyone else seemed to be writing and having no troubles."

- "I loved this activity. I grew up speaking two languages. I rarely get a chance to express myself in my home language. As I started writing, I had a flood of memories from my childhood."

- "I didn't want you to see it. I felt so unintelligent. Silenced, frustrated, angry, dumb, ashamed."

Writing in a Second Language Is Unique

Writing in a first language, which is the norm for many monolingual students and ELA teachers in the United States, differs from the cognitive and academic demands of writing in a second language, which is the challenge for most ELL students in ELA classrooms. Most ELA teachers I've worked with over the years seem to intuitively understand the difficulty their multilingual/ELL students face when writing in English. They know that it must be difficult. They see many of their students struggle. They may hark back to memories of studying abroad or taking a test in a Spanish class many years earlier. But when asked what exactly makes it so difficult or what might make it easier, most teachers aren't sure. So let's begin with this: what exactly makes writing in a second language so difficult?

Recently, I heard a person hypothesize that if English language learners had stronger English vocabulary, knew the right grammatical structures, and knew the rules and punctuation, they could write well. He rationalized that if we just taught certain building blocks—in his opinion, grammar and vocabulary—and these were in place, then writing in a second language would be easy, almost like a kind of plug-and-play game that anyone could master. Plug in the right word, add the right verb tense, and *voilà*! But writing well in a second language requires much more; it's not only about learning a set of technical tools, rules, or vocabulary.

First, let's consider the demands of writing more generally. The cognitive demands of writing are many: getting ideas into words and on paper, understanding a given genre and its conventions, thinking through word choices and mechanics, trying to determine whether the writing is "right" or if the reader will like it, and so on. These demands affect most of our students, regardless of their language backgrounds. In my twenty years of teaching writing at all levels from middle school to high school to college, I've noticed that most students—and even some teachers—see writing as a daunting task, sometimes a risky and possibly embarrassing one. Even those adults and students who are considered successful and talented writers have moments of severe doubt or hesitancy about the words they commit to the page. Now imagine all those cognitive demands doubled—quadrupled—as you navigate creative and academic writing tasks in a second or third language: translating, cross-checking word choices and verb forms, having the word or thought in one language but being unable to find the equivalent meaning or even depth of your ideas in your second language, losing track of one idea as you chase down the language for another. ELL students often tell me that nothing makes them feel as unintelligent and juvenile as having to write in English. On one recent occasion, a student pointed to his beautiful script in Arabic, noting the fluidity with which he wrote passage after passage of poetry and prose, and then compared it to his stilted English block letters, the few short sentences uneven and full of crossed-out words: "It looks like a first grader [wrote it]. In English, I feel that way. So I write when I have to, that is it."

The Research

Students' Writing Process

In 1993, Tony Silva, a leading second language writing researcher, examined more than twenty years of studies on students writing in their second languages, looking for common findings and common student concerns. The research overwhelmingly found that writing in a second language:

- Takes more time.
- Is more cognitively demanding, requiring the writer to shift across languages, new vocabulary or language rules, and cultural expectations of writing. Often these shifts are recursive, with writers drawing on past experiences with language and writing in order to push forward with the new text in front of them.
- Is more labor-intensive. ELL and multilingual writers may spend more time searching for words and developing their thoughts on the page. For some students whose first language uses a different alphabet or logographic system

(e.g., Arabic, Chinese), the process of writing out English words or even typing them can be less fluid, and they feel as though they are writing in starts and stops. Arabic texts, for example, are read from right to left, and they are written in a cursive script. In addition, no distinctions are made between upper- and lowercase.

Many of these factors add up, complicate confidence, and are incredibly time-consuming. Most ELL writers find they are often facing the clock and putting in double and triple the amount of work time their peers take to complete English compositions, responses, and reports. For student writers, the cost of this additional time is evident in fewer revisions, a "What's next?" approach to writing, and a hesitancy to explore beyond set forms or graphic organizers.

Many teachers comment that the compositions of ELL writers tend to be much shorter than those of their monolingual English-speaking peers. In part, this is a direct outcome of the time and labor factors already mentioned. Many ELL writers note that they feel stilted and emotionally disrupted by not being able to express themselves in English as fully as they can in their first language. This frustration is often exacerbated when ELL writers have few strategies for how to "do" revision, especially with more content- and audience-based revisions and planning.

"Good Writing" and the Role of Culture

How do teachers decide what "good writing" is? We have rubrics, standards, samples of past student papers, the input of our colleagues, writing samples from testing and textbook publishers, and the instruction of our own teachers and professors over the years. We also recognize good writing from our reading—books, essays, poetry, op-ed pieces in national papers, magazines, plays both written and performed, pieces we've read through school or for pleasure, and those we've shared with our students. These experiences have all shaped our tastes and the ways we judge a piece of writing: effective or ineffective, organized or disorganized, clear or imprecise, evocative or off-putting, beautiful or plain.

But these tastes and barometers of good writing are not universal. Rarely do we as writing teachers think about how some of these tastes and expectations are shaped and how many of our expectations about genre, form, citation, use of the personal, use of research or secondary sources, among other conventions, are driven by our national and cultural contexts. In many ways, our expectations as teachers reflect a unique American vantage point and educational experience.

We don't often think about the ways in which we define good writing as culturally influenced. However, structures and expectations for "good writing" or "good argument" or "a good narrative" can differ from one nation to the next (Hinds, 1987; Matsuda, 1997; Connor, 2011). For example, Li (2005) studied teachers' responses to student writing, comparing ranking and comments from both Chinese teachers and English teachers. She found that the variations in what was deemed "good writing" were often based on cultural expectations and literacy experiences in the teachers' first language (including past schooling, past feedback that teachers had received from their teachers and professors, and oral and written language uses).

Why is this so? Research on contrastive rhetoric suggests that other countries and cultures may value different rhetorical strategies and patterns from those valued in the United States, particularly for genres such as argument or narrative (Connor, 1996; Matsuda 1997). The problem is that we often teach these genre expectations as though they were universal. But readers' expectations are not universal. Our expectations as readers are bound up in our cultures, our own educational experiences, and the texts we've seen. In some cultures, for example, it's assumed that readers will take more responsibility in extracting information and understanding the writer's intent. A study conducted by George Mason University found that many international students were "confused about why their teachers in the U.S. placed so much emphasis on structuring a paper, including having an explicit thesis and topic sentences. For many, this confusion stems from their experiences writing within 'reader-responsible' cultures" (Zawacki, Hajabbasi, Habib, & Das, 2007).

In an influential study, John Hinds (1987) defined "reader-responsible" languages as those that place the burden on readers for extracting meaning from the text. In some Asian cultures, for instance, readers expect and are comfortable with a certain level of ambiguity or even a delayed thesis; readers learn to move inductively through a text. In contrast, American academic writing tends to reflect a more writer-responsible culture, in which English-speaking readers learn, and teachers teach, that "good writing" is explicit and direct. In practice, this kind of writer-responsible style pushes us to expect the writer's thesis or focus to appear earlier in a text. Similarly, this American academic style encourages teachers to teach that topic sentences should focus paragraphs and that each paragraph should include certain types of evidence. Even rules about citation, plagiarism, and textual ownership are influenced by culture, and these vary even among traditionally English-dominant countries (Currie, 1998). In our work with student writers, we rarely acknowledge the differences between English in closely linked countries such as the United States and the United Kingdom, differences that are evident in the varying expectations around citation, grammar, idioms, and spelling.

My own multilingual students have often noted the strangeness of American readers' expectations of writers, pointing out that the United States seems to require a high level of clarity and forthrightness in order to understand a text. They are often confused by the extensive attention paid to citation and style rules. They may have learned different patterns of organization for cohesive and persuasive arguments. Even multilingual students who have not formally studied writing in their home languages may still be influenced by storytelling traditions and patterns of argument they see used in their communities, read in home language poetry and novels, and hear among extended family.

The reality is that many English teachers are influenced by a "myth of linguistic homogeneity," a general assumption that all students are English dominant and that certain standards and conventions about English writing, or writing more generally, are universal (Matsuda, 1997, 2006). When English teachers encounter student writing that doesn't seem to follow US-based cultural norms or conventions, they may judge these student essays as off-putting or lacking clarity. We often fail to see a student's work through the lens of alternative rhetorical strategies, or, worse, we jump to the conclusion that the student's thinking is unclear, rather than considering that the student writer is drawing on other cultural ideas of "good writing," "good argument," and "good storytelling."

At the same time, it's important to acknowledge that people aren't simply products of their nations. A whole range of past experiences with reading, writing, and literacy in general influences multilingual student writers. In other words, we can't just assume that all Asian or all Latino/a students, for example, write in the same way. Cultures within countries are not homogeneous; regional differences are common. Previous education, and even the ways in which national education policy impact curricula or testing, can also play a large role in how students approach writing tasks. Matsuda (1997, 2006) has suggested that we as teachers consider our own assumptions and biases before we read the texts of ELL/multilingual writers, noting that we need to find a bidirectional middle ground, mediated by working with the student and the student's texts. We should consider how the students' previous language, writing, and educational experiences may impact their ideas about good writing. We also need to become more accepting of the different rhetorical approaches and traditions that our multilingual students bring to their work. At the same time, Matsuda recommends that we turn a mirror on ourselves as readers. We need to consider and reflect on how our own language background, writing experiences, and previous teachers and training impact how we read and respond to the texts of multilingual writers. When reading and evaluating the effectiveness of a multilingual student's writing, we can often be more open to that student's ideas, innovations, effective language, and rhetorical strengths if we are cognizant that many of our judgments about good writing are bound up in a specific culture and taste, influenced by our educational systems and our own past literacy experiences.

Recognizing the Sociocultural Factors of ELL Writing

Writing is always socially situated. So are writers, especially immigrant, refugee, and resident bilingual students in our schools. Linguist Ken Hyland (2009) explains that writing in a second language involves studying linguistic features, but he also notes the importance of cultural aspects of writing practices like those discussed previously. In addition, he identifies the sociopolitical and identity factors that shape multilingual students' perceptions, motivations, classroom participation, and English writing experiences. Our multilingual students may be wrestling with writing in English or figuring out an assignment, but at the same time they may also be asking themselves: Who am I? How do I want to be seen by my peers? By my friends? By my teachers? By my parents? Do I want to share my language background? What does my writing tell others about me? Does it make me feel like an insider or an outsider? Which social groups do I want to be a part of? How do my school and classroom performance make my peers or friends see me? Identity factors are particularly salient when teachers are working with adolescent writers, who are often dealing with the complexities of figuring out who they are, who they want to be grouped with, and how they want to be seen by peers, teachers, and family members. And students are often shifting their answers to these questions or finding themselves in conflict about how they want to be seen and understood by the various stakeholders in their lives. For many multilingual teenagers, this identity work occurs at the same time that they are developing their literacies, and that reality can make writing and learning to write in English much more complicated (Ortmeier-Hooper & Enright, 2011).

Likewise, many bilingual and immigrant students may be attuned to contentious political and community discussions on English-only and immigration policies. Race, language, and competing definitions of "Who is American?" permeate their communities, television and radio programs, and the broader US cultural and political landscape. Students who are aware of these discussions often feel like targets in their towns, cities, and schools if they dare to speak, reveal their accents, or use their home languages. In some situations and places, their sense of being targeted is quite real. For example, in the aftermath of the 2016 presidential election, bilingual and refugee students in many schools faced an uptick in brazen bullying, along with subtle and not-so-subtle threats. Teachers told stories of refugee children being taunted, asked by their peers if they were terrorists. In some cities, graffiti written on the sides of walls suggested that immigrants should go home. In one city, police reports revealed that graffiti was found written on the side of an apartment door that housed a young immigrant family, telling them to leave or they would be harmed. Such incidents create a very real sense of fear, and at times antipathy among students to using the English language. They question why they should join a language community that seems so hostile or inhospitable. Still other students respond to these discussions and incidents by becoming politically active, and with the help of a supportive community and teachers, they learn to use their skills in English and other languages to speak out against xenophobic speech and policies that are hurtful to their friends and families.

In terms of school identities, multilingual students may interpret their linguistic diversity as a strength or as something that singles them out. Some may love having opportunities to share stories from home cultures and the countries with which they are familiar. Others will try to blend in with the monolingual, English-speaking kids in the room. Students may resent being classified only in terms of their language and classrooms if their teachers box them into ELL categories in ways that nullify their other achievements and identities: cheerleader, honor society member, yearbook editor, actor, soccer player, student journalist, poet.

How adolescents negotiate these kinds of identity situations is often directly or indirectly linked to their efforts in the writing classroom. Some ELLs may be reluctant to take part in peer review or share their writing with peers, even those who are friends. Others may resent using English because it builds a kind of linguistic wall between them and members of their families. Learning something about the kinds of identity negotiations that are shaping multilingual students can help teachers make decisions about how to approach these student writers and writing instruction. For instance, literacy researcher Danling Fu (2009) notes that ELL writers may find that returning to strategies they have used for writing in their first language (whether writing personally, online, or in their first language schools) can be helpful when writing in English.

Cycles of Inopportunity

The difficulties of writing in a second language are further compounded by lack of practice and lack of sustained training in how to develop a piece of writing. The writing practice that ELLs and multilinguals receive in US classrooms and the writing curriculum they experience are often incredibly narrow. Studies comparing

ELL students' experiences in lower-level and upper-level academic tracks in ELA and science classrooms have found that ELL students stuck in lower-level tracks have few opportunities for sustained and meaningful writing; instead, their writing experiences are often limited to graphic organizers, short paragraph practice, single-sentence responses, worksheets, and only the most basic of writing instruction (Fu, 1995; Enright, 2010; Enright & Gilliland, 2011; Ruecker, 2015). As I have argued elsewhere, opportunities for ELL writers to pursue rich, meaningful, project-based or inquiry-based writing instruction and sustained writing practice are often inadequate or cut short due to competing curricular demands (Ortmeier-Hooper, 2013). In addition, many teachers have not been trained to work with the writing of ELL/multilingual students (Larsen, 2013).

Given how little practice these students have been given and how few writing strategies they have been taught, it's no wonder they lack confidence and try to hide from writing activities. Some of my former students have identified shorter compositions as a writing strategy, noting that when they write shorter compositions, there are few chances for error. Some ELL writers rationalize that they can correct their writing better by keeping it contained to a certain length, using simpler sentence and paragraph structures, and not taking chances with vocabulary and word choice. Students rationalize (often correctly) that these strategies contain fewer risks, and they are less likely to be marked down for errors. Students correctly think through the cost-benefit analysis:

> more errors = lower grades
>
> lower grades = fewer opportunities to advance
>
> low grades + failing to succeed = no college

In this light, we can sympathize with students' efforts to avoid writing or, at the very least, to escape a writing assignment with the fewest red marks possible.

Meeting the Needs of ELL Writers: Adding to Your Repertoire as an ELA/Writing Teacher and Why It Matters

In 2011, Kerry Enright, a teacher educator from the University of California, Davis, wrote that the "new mainstream" classroom in the twenty-first century includes more and more linguistically and culturally diverse students. Diversity is becoming the norm. As Randy Bomer (2005), former president of the National Council of Teachers of English (NCTE), noted, "We [as ELA teachers] can no longer be content with saying, 'the ESL teacher will take care of all those kids'" (16)

Because the writing needs of ELL students are unique, mainstream teachers will need to add to their instructional repertoire in order to help students make definitive strides as writers within these demographically diverse and linguistically rich "new mainstream" classrooms. Some of what I discuss in this book will look familiar to many ELA teachers, but certain strategies embedded in these practices have particular benefits for the ELL/multilingual writers in the room. Other suggestions and practices are more overtly specific to these writers. Teacher response and assessment is one such area. Overall, though, I approach best practices for working with ELL and multilingual writers from a universal design approach, meaning that most of what I have learned over the years about working with diverse learners has led to better practices for all of my student writers, monolingual and multilingual.

What is at stake? In most US high schools, very few multilingual and ELL students gain access to upper-level college preparatory classes. Even if ELL students are exited from ELL programs or pass language proficiency exams to enter mainstream classes, they often find themselves placed in lower-level academic tracks. Research confirms that ELLs often have limited opportunities to participate in high-level academic curricula in US schools (Enright & Gilliland, 2011; Kanno & Kangas, 2014). Even when these courses are available through an open application process, many multilingual students are too intimidated to apply, worried about a lack of support and often discouraged by teachers and guidance counselors. Many English language learners are just grateful to get enough ELA credits to graduate from high school. And many ELLs and their parents wrongly assume that all ELA courses are considered equal in the selection process for colleges and universities.

Some teachers and administrators assume that if students can graduate, they will find success and more remedial services at local community colleges, considering them like a thirteenth year of high school. But the statistics on these students' attrition rates at two-year colleges are alarming. Difficulties and lack of confidence with college-level reading and writing are often part of the problem. Overall, recent studies based on statistical analyses suggest that ELLs' access to postsecondary education is limited in comparison to that of their non-ELL peers. Kanno and Kangas (2014) report that in 2006, only 19 percent of ELLs advanced to four-year institutions. Given the high stakes around multilingual writing and ELL adolescents, we have to begin to translate research into classroom practice.

In the following chapters, I build on our knowledge of ELL/multilingual students and writing in order to consider several important components to working with these writers in English classrooms. Throughout, I share stories of students I've worked with through my research and teaching. I consider the challenges teachers face as they try to improve instruction, engagement, and student writing, and I also offer evidence-based strategies for responding to and evaluating multilingual writers and their texts. In particular, I am fortunate to have worked closely with teachers as we explored and enacted many of the techniques and strategies discussed in this book. Mrs. Keller,[1] an English and ELL teacher, is one such educator; her classroom is featured as an ongoing example of some of the strategies and methods shared in this volume. The activities featuring Mrs. Keller took place in urban high school classrooms with high numbers of linguistically diverse writers, ages fourteen to eighteen. I explore the possibilities that Mrs. Keller, the other teachers, and I gained from focusing on the strengths of ELL/multilingual student writers. Chapters 3, 4, and 5 then explore best practices for developing explicit writing strategies and instructional techniques. Specifically, these chapters look at ways to design assignments (Chapter 3), methods for teaching writing explicitly (Chapter 4), and approaches to responding to ELL writers and texts (Chapter 5). In Chapter 6, I look more broadly at assessment practices, considering what is fair and equitable assessment for multilingual writers. Finally, in Chapter 7, I connect this work to issues of social justice, calling on this work as a way to change the cycle of inopportunity.

But before we get to those more hands-on examples, Chapter 2 begins with a focus on globalization and new trends in 21st century literacies, both of which are causing fundamental shifts in our perceptions about writing, readers, English users, and multilingual students.

A note as you delve into the next chapters: You'll have seen already in this chapter that I use many acronyms and terms when referring to multilingual students—a variation in naming that is prevalent across the field. The authors of the four books in the Principles in Practice imprint concerning teaching English language learners have worked together to create some consistency in naming and some explanation of what we mean by the terms. See the statement of terminology and glossary on pages xix–xxii for definitions of some of the most current terms.

**Chapter
Two**

A Changing World: How Globalization Helps Us See the Strengths of ELL Writers in New Ways

Ahmed's Story

Ahmed sits in a classroom in New Hampshire. He is an Iraqi, a refugee of the war-torn country, and his father was an ally of the US military there. Ahmed's mother, cousins, and siblings left Iraq one night, escaping to Jordan and then to Turkey. They lived in Turkey for a number of years before being approved for refugee resettlement in the United States. In conversations, Ahmed explains that he often feels more Turkish than Iraqi and, as of late, more American than Turkish. During a break from his high school classes, he has his iPhone within reach, and sometimes he is found texting to friends and cousins in Turkey. Sometimes the texts are in English; other times they are in Turkish. Some mornings he reports that he and his family spoke via Skype the night before with a cousin who remains in a terrorist-controlled part of Iraq. Ahmed is studying for the SATs, learning English vocabulary, and speaks daily of his desire to go to a good college. He wants to study business and engineering. At fifteen years old, he is literate and fluent in Arabic, Turkish, and now English.

I tell Ahmed's story in order to capture how aspects of his experiences reflect significant world phenomena occurring as a result of globalization in the twenty-first century. Specifically, Ahmed's journeys and circumstances give us a window into aspects of connectivity, language learning and global Englishes, transnational migration, and the ways in which technology is facilitating interconnectivity and interdependence across a range of literacy activities. They also provide a window into understanding the kinds of strengths that ELL writers bring to ELA classrooms.

In this chapter, I explore how globalization and transnationalism are shifting the ways in which we understand English as a global language, the ways we teach writing, and the ways we see and recognize the strengths of our ELL/multilingual writers. The chapter opens with some thoughts on how we can build globalized classrooms that foster and accentuate the strengths and gifts of ELL writers, while at the same time fostering a more global understanding of writing among all our students. I then explore ways for teachers to learn more about the linguistic and rhetorical strengths that individual writers bring into their classrooms.

Creating Classrooms That Accentuate the Strengths of ELL Writers

Globalization and the ELA Classroom

> Students appreciate that the twenty-first-century classroom and workplace are settings in which people from often widely divergent cultures and who represent diverse experiences and perspectives must learn and work together. Students actively seek to understand other perspectives and cultures through reading and listening, and they are able to communicate effectively with people of varied backgrounds.
>
> —Common Core State Standards Initiative (2010, p. 7)

> As the world becomes more complex, increasingly flattened, and, one might argue, ever more interesting and challenging, our students must be prepared to enter it as competent, thoughtful, and agentive readers and communicators.
>
> —National Council of Teachers of English (2007)

NCTE has defined *globalization* as "the expanding connectivity, integration, and interdependence of economic, social, technological, cultural, political, and ecological spheres across local activities" (NCTE, 2007). Increasingly, the students in ELA classrooms need to be prepared to enter a globalized society in which they will be called on to communicate across a range of linguistic and cultural boundaries in their personal, academic, and work lives. The current CCSS movement echoes these interests by stressing "international benchmarks." Likewise, we often hear educators, administrators, and parents discuss the mastery of skills needed in a "globally competitive" society. In the CCSS, the Standards for English Language

What Does It Mean to Be "Transnational"?

The twenty-first century is quickly becoming a century of massive movement of people within nations and across national borders. The United Nations suggests that more than 190 million people worldwide can be classified as transnational migrants (UN Department of Economic and Social Affairs, 2005). Some individuals, classified as migrants, are similar to Ahmed, whose story opens this chapter. Migrants like Ahmed are displaced by war, political strife, and economic uncertainty. They often transverse various nations as they strive to find stability, and they often they settle in countries like the United States as refugees. But other transnational families are led to new countries by their jobs, following positions at large multinational firms that seek to expand into global markets. Still others follow family or educational opportunities. Transnationals like Ahmed can also be the sons and daughters of immigrants residing in the United States, but they are individuals who continue to hold on to strong relationships with family and friends in other nations through the power of the Internet and other technology. These young people are developing more transnational identities and languages by communicating with cousins, other family members, and friends in their parents' countries via Skype, smartphones, and social media. They see the world as much more integrated and connected than immigrants of the early nineteenth and twentieth centuries did. These transnational trends are mirrored, in part, by multinational trends in business, science and technology research, health care, politics, and the growing use of English as an international language (EIL) in writing, speaking, and reading.

Arts and Literacy note that students "need wide, deep and thoughtful engagement with literary and informational texts that build knowledge, enlarge experience, and *broaden worldviews*" (CCSSI, 2010, p. 3, my emphasis).

Despite the growing acknowledgment that teachers need to attend to globalization in their ELA teaching, the calls for a more globalized perspective are often not intertwined with discussions of ELL/multilingual writers in our schools—and they should be. For one, the ELL writers in our classes can provide useful insights into how their monolingual peers might learn to navigate across language, cultural, and other differences.

English as an International Language

These days, English is an international lingua franca, shared and used by many in politics, humanitarian efforts, and the economy. For example, in 2009 there were more than 300 million Chinese speakers of English, and that number continues to grow. English is no longer "owned" solely by those in what have been traditionally seen as "native-English-speaking" countries such as the United States, Canada, the United Kingdom, and Australia. Learning and using English as an international language has become the norm across many nations. In many countries, learning and using English on a daily basis is like getting a driver's license, a high school diploma, or a passport (You, 2010).

But the Englishes (and yes, I use the plural with purpose here) used in these settings may sound quite different from US English spoken by monolingual students—and in ways beyond an accent. Linguists, often working in the field of World Englishes and applied linguistics, study the changes in English as it becomes an international language, documenting and comparing the emerging varieties of English such as Chinese English and Nigerian

English, among others. Speakers of English in more traditional English-speaking countries, like the United States, are often surprised to learn about changes in the conventions, expectations, and usage that are part of these Englishes. But this isn't just an academic exercise. To understand how transnational and global these varieties of English have become, all you need to do is pick up an iPhone. Siri, the intelligent personal assistant software built into the phone's operating system, has language setting preferences that include Singaporean English, among others. Phrases such as "catch no ball" (meaning "I don't understand") and "one leg kick" (meaning "to do something by oneself") are not marked as errors by Siri or others using Singaporean English in oral communication and in print.

Toward Broader Understandings of Communicative and Writing Competence

I teach in New Hampshire, and most of the teachers and students I work with aren't thinking about the global scale of English. Some of my students have never left our state, even though Boston, Massachusetts, is only an hour-long car ride away. But the movement toward English as an international language, along with heightened uses of technology, has implications for our teaching and for students in our ELA classrooms, even those who don't yet see themselves as part of the global picture. For one, US students today are more likely to live in a world and enter a workplace that includes contact time with more international users of English. It is a world that requires us as English teachers to (re)consider standards and objectives for English *communicative competence* for not only ELLs but also monolinguals in the secondary ELA classroom. For many of our secondary students, the idea of a globalized citizenry, university, and workforce will seem irrelevant; college and the workplace can feel far removed from students' daily realities, pursuits that exist in a distant future that they cannot imagine. But as secondary ELA teachers, we can begin to lay the groundwork for shifting student attitudes and dispositions to help them imagine the globalized world they are entering and begin to foster the communicative competencies that will prepare them for what lies ahead (Canagarajah, 2013).

One by-product of such a shift is the potential to create a far more open and receptive classroom community (and even curriculum) for ELL/multilingual students, who often feel that their diverse language understandings, knowledge of cross-cultural language practices, and transnational experiences work against them and place them on the margins when it comes to writing in the ELA classroom. Such shifts can create moments in which the ELL/multilingual writers in the room get to enter assignments, discussions, and projects from a standpoint of expertise, authority, and communicative competence that actually benefits the entire classroom community.

Matsuda and Hammill (2014) explain that *"communicative competence* involves not only the knowledge and discourse but also the awareness of appropriate ways of creating and maintaining social relationships with the audience as well as the strategic knowledge, such as the knowledge of writing processes" (p. 269). Not all ELL/multilingual students will have the same degree of communicative competence; various factors influence the depth and breadth of communicative competence students have or are aware of. Multilingual students are affected by their individual second language backgrounds, age of language learning, and level of metalinguistic knowledge and awareness (Ortega, 2014). But even with this variability, many ELL and multilingual teens have had experiences that provide them with a stronger strategic sense of how to communicate and maintain social relationships with various groups—across language, age, and socioeconomic status.

Communicative competence also has implications for students we have traditionally thought of as "mainstream." Driven by the global economy, technology and the Internet, and the ease of travel and relocation across borders due to work or study, we are entering an era in which learning additional languages is quickly becoming the global norm, and the ability to move back and forth between languages and across cultural norms is becoming an important skill. Former Assistant Secretary of State for Educational and Cultural Affairs Evan Ryan notes that "only by engaging multiple perspectives within our societies can we all reap the numerous benefits of international education—increased global competence, self-awareness and resiliency, and the ability to compete in the 21st century economy" (Institute of International Education and US Department of State Bureau of Educational and Cultural Affairs, 2014). Some scholars, like linguist Stephen May (2013), have defined this as the era of the "multilingual turn," a time in which multilingualism, communicative competence, and cross-cultural experiences are becoming the hallmark of a good education. For monolingual English-speaking students, the goal of communicative competence is often complicated by a lack of meaningful interaction with multilinguals, a US-centric view of English, an uncertainty about how to create social relationships with readers and audiences across cultural boundaries, and a limited awareness of how language users negotiate meaning in writing.

Many of our multilingual students negotiate these kinds of dynamic language situations on a daily basis. In the hallways of his school, Ahmed shouts out to a friend on the soccer team in Arabic, then turns to another teammate and asks in English about the upcoming game schedule. On his cell phone, he listens to Kanye West and reads a BuzzFeed post on the latest Batman movie. When he heads home, he will stop at the local convenience store to pick up a Mountain Dew, murmuring *"Gracias"* to the clerk. Then he will pass by the houses of neighbors, speaking to them in Turkish and English. Once home, his father may ask him to come along to the car mechanic to help translate and even negotiate the payment transaction in English, or he may go with his grandmother to the dentist's office to help fill out paperwork, again acting as a translator for his family. When he returns home, he will watch Telemundo with his uncle as they cheer for their favorite soccer team. He will practice his prayers and read in Arabic. As he walks through his day, Ahmed is displaying the kinds of language prowess and negotiating skills that he has learned and continues to polish as a multilingual speaker. Even in written language, he will make choices about composing in English or Arabic, formal or informal, emoji or standard text, depending on his readers and his purposes.

In contrast, there are students in Ahmed's school and some of his classes who are monolingual and lack Ahmed's level of communicative competence. They don't have the kinds of language experiences Ahmed lives daily. Until recently, this was accepted as the norm. But most of today's US students will grow up and head out into the larger world where more and more people will be well versed in communicating across languages and cultures. Given these trends, Ahmed's communicative strengths, his insights, and his inherent knowledge of language negotiation should be seen as an important asset, not just for Ahmed but also for his teacher and his peers.

Global English and College- and Career-Readiness

For many of our students, more global and transnational experiences will begin as soon as they enter local US colleges and universities. Every year we see more and more students entering higher education. Increasingly, they will be in classes with and work alongside the high numbers of international students who come to study here. In 2014, for example, more than 885,000 international students were studying in US colleges and universities (Institute, 2014). That number continues to rise. These students are not coming as part of one- or two-semester exchange programs. Instead, they are matriculating into two- and four-year college degree programs, as well as graduate programs. US colleges and universities—from community colleges to state universities to the Ivy Leagues—have become the top destination for university study for students around the world. In addition, international students bring more than 27 million dollars into the US economy each year (Haynie, 2014).

In the workplace there is a similar trend toward a more global, transnational workforce. Growing numbers of employers in industry and commerce are reflecting economic trends by engaging in multinational business ventures, import-export dealings, and transnational cooperation. More and more employers are using English, but business employers are also placing high importance on second language skills. Aided by an increase in transnational commerce, global economy, and international trade, multilingualism, international education, and cross-cultural competences are highly valued in the workplace. As one Fortune 400-spokesperson noted, "The aim is to hire globally and to place globally. Knowledge of more than one language demonstrates that a candidate has the ability to think across cultural boundaries" (Didiot-Cook, Gauthier, & Scheirlinckx, 2000). As the NCTE report on globalization explains, "While one might effectively argue that teaching standard English remains important for formal or business communication, it is also fair to say that English is becoming more complex than ever, and our students will need to be flexible and efficient users of a vast array of discourses" (NCTE, 2007).

Why Should Ahmed's Experiences Matter to His Peers?

Currently, US native-born English speakers are unlikely to have international and positive cross-cultural experiences that enhance their abilities to communicate in savvy ways across cultural boundaries. US students are less likely to travel abroad than their peers in other nations, and in spite of foreign language classes or because they are avoiding foreign language training altogether, increasingly they see themselves as happily monolingual. Many question whether learning a second language is necessary and argue that it is too difficult. And in their daily lives, many monolingual US students have fewer structured and positive cross-cultural interactions as part of their educational development. A lack of cross-cultural experience and education means that many students lack the sensitivity and knowledge necessary to respond to and work alongside individuals with different cultural assumptions, and they are less agile when participating in the kinds of intercultural communication that are needed in many workplaces. As teachers, however, we can begin to create curriculum and classroom activities that challenge all of our students to think more broadly and globally about language, writing, and even research.

In the Classroom

Building in Transnational Perspectives through Research and Writing

The remainder of this chapter considers a number of ways to incorporate more transnational and worldly perspectives on English use into the ELA classroom. Here, I start with an activity designed to bring together reading, writing, and research skills. This exercise, developed by Joleen Hanson (2013) at the University of Wisconsin-Stout, is a research activity that strives to help all ELA students "learn strategies for moving out of their monolingual comfort zones and negotiating language difference in a multilingual world" (p. 207). The goal is to provide an avenue for ELL/multilingual writers to share their expertise in other languages and non-English-based resources with their peers. At the same time, this activity is designed to expand ELA teachers' expectations of not only the ELL/multilingual students in our classrooms, but also of our monolingual English students. Students are grouped together, three to four students to a group, to investigate a research question or topic using Internet searches and non-English websites to begin to understand global and multilingual perspectives on their topic.

In class, students use alternative Google sites based in different countries—from Canada to Mexico to Ghana to Germany (i.e., www. Google.ca, www. Google.mx, etc.)—and enter search terms from their research topic. They might also use non-English sources based in the United States, such as community newspapers and websites aimed at a specific local language community in their state. Once students have located a website or two using their search terms, student teams begin making observations about the site and its content, which they will later have translated.

Hanson (2013) asks student groups to write out their observations on the page's organization, graphics, and text to see how much they can learn from visual deduction. Students then cut and paste text from the website into Google Translate in order to identify whether the content of the page was truly related to their topic and how. What do they observe about the writing, the content, and the perspective presented? The translation allows students to determine whether their initial deductions were correct, as well as what they might have missed. Students then write and report on what they observed and learned from the activity.

Other variations of this assignment include having students compare and discuss newspapers and news websites from other countries but written in English. News organization sites, such as *Deutsche Welle, The Rio Times, The Guardian Nigeria, China Daily, Yucatan Times, The Argentina Independent*, provide provocative opportunities for US high school students to see how the arts (movies and music), artists, current events, political figures, and even popular culture are written about and reviewed in other parts of the world. Another great source is the Newseum website, http://www.newseum.org/todaysfrontpages/?tfp_display=gallery&tfp_region=International&tfp_sort_by=country, which shares the front pages of articles and newspapers from around the world. Teachers can have students consider which stories get the major headlines in other countries, how US news stories are reported, and what they notice about the genres, language use, and formats of the websites.

Hanson (2013) admits that many monolingual English students in her writing classrooms are initially resistant to this activity. She spends time discussing the activity's relevance to their work as thinkers and readers. She also discusses the importance of a broader worldview by pointing to future workplace expectations, American companies with multinational employees and customers, and the changing expectations in higher education. As she explains, these kinds of activities operate on the assumption that "writing teachers need to help all students, but particularly those who function only in English, to gain fluency in working across language differences in all features of written language" (p. 207). From the perspective of the ELL/multilingual writers in the classroom, these kinds of activities provide unique opportunities for them to demonstrate their expertise on crossing cultural and language boundaries. These activities also legitimize ELL/multilingual students' resources from their home communities and showcase these students' critical thinking skills and heightened sensitivities toward how individuals and news agencies communicate across cultures.

Recognizing the Strengths of Ahmed and the ELL Writers in Your Classroom

Tapping into the Strengths of ELL/Multilingual Writers in the ELA Classroom

Ahmed reports to me that he often sits in the back of his ELA classroom. He hasn't talked about his knowledge of Arabic to his teacher, and he isn't quite sure how it would matter or why she would care. It is an *English* class, after all. He says that he likes the anonymity, but as we talk further, I learn that he has started to embrace the anonymity because he really doesn't see any other choice. His ELA teacher doesn't seem to want to get to know him, and the other students in the class aren't all that interested in his experiences or language abilities. So he sits in the back, attentive but silent. Sadly, his ELA teacher isn't aware that he feels this way. Even though she works with a high number of students each day, she has noticed Ahmed in the back. She is wondering what his story is, but at the same time, she's worried that if she asks too much he might feel singled out or offended.

Unfortunately, many of the literacy experiences and cross-cultural competencies that ELL/multilingual writers bring to their classrooms remain hidden from ELA teachers. Students are afraid to share them. They aren't sure that their experiences across languages actually have value. They rarely see an opportunity or receive an invitation from teachers outside of the ELL classroom to bring these strengths to their work as readers, writers, and communicators. Likewise, teachers often explain that they don't speak their ELL students' home languages, or that they aren't sure how they can tap into those backgrounds and literacy experiences in the classroom if they don't speak the languages of their students.

In the final section of this chapter, I share some ideas for activities that create opportunities for ELL/multilingual writers to reveal some of their interests, strengths, aspirations, and activities so that teachers can have a stronger sense of the competencies and literacy experiences students are bringing with them. I also offer up some activities for creating more opportunities for all the students in our classes to develop multilingual and global perspectives.

In the Classroom

Mapping and Manipulatives: Learning about Students' Literacies, Interests, and Aspirations

In my work as a teacher and adolescent literacy researcher, I often find that middle and high school students are unsure and a bit suspicious of teachers' direct questions about their literacy backgrounds. Quite simply, they don't know what we want to know or why it's relevant. With English language learners, answers to these kinds of questions are often difficult to elicit, not only because of students' uncertainty about relevance, but also because of their lack of confidence in expressing the depth or expansiveness of their literacy experiences and relationships in English. The following activity is a modification of a research tool that I developed to talk with adolescent multilingual writers about their work as writers, along with the people, books, authors, popular media, and even places that they saw as some way sponsoring their literacies (Ortmeier-Hooper, 2013; Brandt, 2001).

When I started working with young multilinguals as part of my first major research project, I was stumped. How could I learn more from these adolescents in a way that didn't feel threatening? How could I help them develop the language to talk about their backgrounds within the framework of big, theoretical concepts such as learning, sponsorship, and literacy? I stumbled on the answer as I watched my son working on his fourth-grade math homework. As I watched my own child use manipulatives (base 10 blocks, fractions strips, beans, geometric solids, etc.) to learn about fractions, I was reminded that math teachers often use tools to teach concepts such as division, fractions, and area. Manipulatives provide students with a strategy to visually represent a concept. When students physically move the objects to show relationships, their senses, particularly sight and touch, are actively engaged. In math the theory on using manipulatives suggests that once students are able to visually represent a concept using tangible objects, they also have greater accessibility to the language they need to describe and explain it. Discussions and learning can also become more focused when students can refer back to the models they've built.

In the ELA classroom, we can draw on the theory of manipulatives to help our students, particularly our English language learners, tell the stories of their literacies and their interests. In this activity, the teacher asks students to use shapes representing

- People—those they know in person or those they have read or heard stories about (e.g., heroes, parents, grandparents, past and present teachers, religious leaders, authors, musicians and artists)

- Groups—in-school and out-of-school communities (e.g., the band, the soccer team, the yearbook, the after-school church group, groups of peers or family, a neighborhood group, a gaming group, an online community or discussion board, etc.)

- Objects—books, movies, diaries or journals, TV shows, games, computers, smartphones, online sites, etc.

- Places—schools (previous and current), after-school programs, sports centers, after-school workplaces, summer workplaces, camps, colleges and universities, churches, mosques, synagogues, websites, the homes of family members or friends

- Events—literacy events that were meaningful to them (e.g., the book I wrote in second grade, my mother reading to me, the time I gave a speech, a piece of music I wrote, the résumé I wrote with the school-to-work program, the poem that the teacher read, my grandmother teaching me a recipe and my translating into English for a friend, an essay or poem that I wrote and the teacher shared with the class as a model, the time I tutored my younger brother, etc.)

Students write out names and labels on the shape icons, with each label briefly describing the person, place, or event that in some way sponsored and encouraged them as students, readers, and writers. Students then take these icons and paste them to a poster board with their name in the center. Teachers ask students to group the icons, placing those with the most influence closest to their names and the center, and those with less influence on the outskirts of the poster. Figures 2.1–2.5 provide some examples. In a variation of this activity, Wight (2015, 2017b) asked students to group icons into Connection or Conflict categories, so that she could get a sense of some of the negative experiences they'd had with literacy and language learning, as well as the positives.

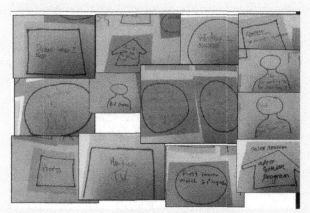

Figure 2.1. Collage of various students' literacy icons.

After students complete their maps, teachers can interview students or have students share their maps in small groups. The students whose work I share here described each item on the map and explained why they placed them where they did. Students who were once hesitant to talk or who previously had answered in one or two words now spoke more confidently. They had a visual artifact they could turn to as they explained how certain people or experiences had shaped them. Their teacher and I noticed that the students found language to talk about their literacies, and they

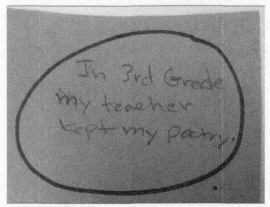

Figure 2.2. "In 3rd Grade my teacher kept my poetry."

Figure 2.3. "[When my] mother Taught [me] how to write [in Spanish]."

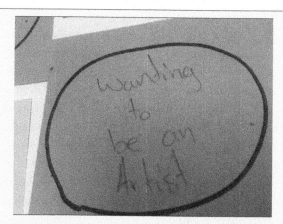

Figure 2.4. "Wanting to be an Artist."

Figure 2.5. "Cousins [. . .] encourages [me] saying you can do it."

in turn began to develop an understanding of literacies and learning that was much broader and more inclusive. We also noted that most multilingual students in the class had aspirations of going to college, wanted to be the first in their families to graduate with a college degree, and were interested in jobs in science, technology, the arts, and more. They were reading biographies, following the career decisions of rap stars and business entrepreneurs, finding inspiration from online news stories, and reading popular books (in their first language and sometimes in English) that were not part of the classroom curriculum. For example, a student's map icons (Figure 2.5) revealed her literary sponsors, including her grandparents and her encouraging cousins. We saw the richness of their literacy lives that had often remained hidden. And as the students saw that their teacher thought these experiences were valuable, they themselves began to recognize the value of these experiences, the richness of their literacies, and how they might begin to connect those experiences to their school lives.

For some students, the mapping activity helped them begin to develop some meta-awareness of how these experiences might be useful in the classroom and in their writing. For her part, their teacher found it valuable to turn back to the students' maps throughout the school year, giving students the opportunity to identify how items on this map might connect to or impact particular writing assignments and educational decisions. Students also had a chance to add icons for new resources and events to their maps at the end of the year.

Translanguaging as a Communicative and Writing Strength

English as an Additional Language

In recent years, the fields of TESOL, applied linguistics, and second language acquisition have started to reexamine some of our commonly held beliefs about how students acquire and add languages to their repertoire. Traditionally, discussions of language learning have taken place within a more monolingual framework. For example, we talk about "English language learning," but we don't often talk about English as an additional language or address ways of maintaining a student's first language. Even in the research on bilingual education, the learning of one language and the maintenance of the student's native language were often discussed in forums different from those that considered English language acquisition. Teachers, and even school administrators and parents, would voice concern that one language might contaminate the other or that issues of language confusion might become a problem for students. But in recent years, research on language learning has considered that people's development and use of languages, especially when they know multiple languages, is much more fluid and integrated. This research has led many teachers and language researchers to consider and embrace a "translanguage" perspective to working with multilingual students.

What Is Translanguaging?

Language educators Ofelia García and Tatyana Kleyn (2016) describe translanguaging as the flexible use of language resources in order to make meaning in our lives and in our complex social and academic worlds. It is a language phenomenon that has been documented among bilingual language users. In my own experience as the American-born child of German immigrants, we often practiced forms of translanguaging. My German mother and father came to the United States with limited English language skills. In my childhood, we regularly moved between German and English in our household. My sisters and I spoke English, then switched to German—often mid-sentence—to ask my mother a question, and then moved back to English. As my father read English newspapers or my mother studied accounting at the local community college, we regularly had the large German-English dictionary on the kitchen table, and my mother's textbooks had German words penciled into the margins as she mastered accounts payable procedures, bank reconciliations, and financial statements. When relatives came to visit, our household became German-dominant, but we often switched to English to clarify points of the conversation for my Scottish aunt, who was learning German.

I'm sure you can imagine this same scenario occurring among the multilingual students in your classroom, but updated to include current technologies: students might speak to relatives in the home language and then pull out their smartphones to search Google in English to make their points or find information they then relay back in Spanish to a grandparent or sibling. Or they watch a telenovela in Spanish while simultaneously reading posts or texting to friends in English on their phones. Many students are fans of hip-hop and pop music from Miami, Brazil, France, and Puerto Rico, regularly listening to singers who mix lyrics in their native languages with hooks written, sung, or rapped in English. García (2012) notes that even on Spanish-language radio shows, callers don't always speak

Spanish, and radio broadcasters regularly switch between Spanish and English as they respond to the calls. At a Red Sox game, I watch as pitcher Daisuke Matsuzaka shouts out congratulations and praise to a fellow teammate in English, and then seconds later turns to sign an autograph and speak in Japanese to a young fan visiting from Tokyo.

Ofelia García (García & Beardsmore, 2011; García & Wei, 2014; García & Kleifgen, 2010) and Suresh Canagarajah (2013) point out that translanguaging is not simply moving from one language code to another; they and other applied linguists observe that multilingual students don't use languages as though they are two separate monolingual codes. In other words, communicating isn't in all Spanish and then all English. Instead, García and other researchers suggest that multilingual students have the ability and capacity to pull from a single, rich linguistic repertoire that brings together all their language resources, and they have learned to deploy those resources in selective, strategic, and effective ways to communicate and meet the needs of their audience and accomplish their aims across a range of situations (García, 2012; Valdés, 2003).

Students who translanguage adapt their language use and make decisions about their language practices based on specific communicative situations. Depending on the communicative situation they find themselves in, these students make strategic, often deliberate language choices in order to improve and enhance communication and understanding for a given audience (García & Kleifgen, 2010). Multilingual students have the unique ability to make meaning across languages and have learned to be strategic about how they use language(s) to engage, persuade, and inform their audiences. Multilingual students have almost instinctively learned how to adapt and shift their language use—vocabulary, tone, language, form of address, formality, etc.—to achieve a desired communicative purpose and to build relationships with their audiences.

Building More Multilingual Acceptance into the Classroom

Songs

When using music as part of your instruction, incorporate songs that have multilingual versions.

Transitions between Activities

Think about signals you can use with students to transition between activities. Talk to multilingual students in your classroom to see if they have suggestions for common phrases you could use to redirect or start a new activity. Have students look up the phrases in Google Translate so that the whole class gets involved.

Group Names

When engaging in group or cooperative learning activities, give multilingual or international names to the groups.

Labels

Consider labeling common items in your classroom in English and in the languages of your students. You can create multilingual labels for common supplies, bookshelves, and bulletin boards. Display multilingual signs and inspirational posters in students' languages.

Greetings and Compliments

Learn greetings in the languages of all your students and use them to start the day. Better still, learn compliments and words of congratulations in the languages of your students and strive to use those compliments as part of your response to written and classroom work.

How Does Translanguaging Connect to Writing?

How can teachers use translanguage perspectives to help students write? What happens to English, especially for those students who still struggle with reading and writing in the classroom?

It is important to realize that new language practices only emerge in an inter-relationship with old language practices. In other words, students learn a second or third language best when they can build on knowledge from their first language. Multilingual students who can consider language practices from one language alongside their language practices in another language are often able to notice and explicitly talk about language and rhetorical features; this kind of awareness is necessary for developing linguistic abilities. In a classroom where the teacher recognizes and accepts translanguaging as a particular talent or intellectual gift of her multilingual students, students are more encouraged to embrace all their language practices as resources for academic advancement, including those in English and those for academic purposes. In practice, this means that teachers are open to students using their first languages in their writing when appropriate and helpful. It also means developing assignments that create spaces for students to creatively engage with their first language literacies and share them with others.

In the Classroom

Assignments That Encourage Students' Multilingual and Multiliterate Identities

Identity Texts

This writing assignment encourages students to create bilingual texts in English and their home language. Identity texts, an assignment designed and written about by Jim Cummins (2005, 2006) and Giampapa (2010), are writing and performance opportunities that allow students to share cultural and linguistic identities. As Cummins notes, identity texts "hold up a mirror to students in which their identities are reflected back in a positive light. When students share identity texts with multiple audiences (peers, teachers, parents, grandparents, sister classes, the media, etc.) they are likely to receive positive feedback and affirmation of self in interaction with these audiences" (2005, p. 150).

In presenting this assignment, teachers ask students to write about certain literacy moments or language experiences that showcase how they have been shaped by their transitions, their families, their home languages, their literacy experiences at home or after school, their positive (or negative) experiences with language learning, and their communities. As Cummins et al. note, these kinds of assignments "present an alternative set of principles for promoting academic engagement among English language learners" (Cummins, Bismilla, Chow, Cohen, Giampapa, Leoni, Sandhu & Sastri, 2005, p. 40). Such assignments embrace "two interrelated propositions: English language learners' cultural knowledge and language abilities in their home language are important resources in enabling academic engagement; and English language learners will engage academically to the extent that instruction affirms their identities and enables them to invest their identities in learning" (p. 2).

When assigning identity texts, encourage students to begin writing initial drafts in whatever language they choose. For many students, this will be the language in which they have a stronger writing ability. For some, this may be their home language, particularly if the memories or individuals described in the piece "do not live in English," as a student once told me, but in the language of the family or community. Overall, the objective should be to create a writing situation in which students can generate and express their ideas and identity stories freely. Students can then work on revising and translating, if they need to, to reach a more mixed audience that might include monolingual English speakers.

Cummins et al. (2005) also encourage teachers to think about developing digital versions of this assignment. Digital versions allow students to use voice recorders and cameras to bring in their own voices, capture the voices of family members, and use pictures to extend their written narratives into a visual format.

Language Biographies

Another assignment is to have students write language biographies in which they describe their experiences in different

Starting Points for Identity Texts

Consider how you might build "identity text" assignments or projects from some of the following prompts:

1. Identity and Literacy Objects: Explore a room that is important to you (e.g., a bedroom, family room, kitchen). What literacy objects do you see (e.g., books, magazines, diaries, lists, chalkboards, signs and sayings, etc.)? Who do these objects belong to? What languages do they represent? How are they used by their owners? If you moved recently, what kinds of written pieces did you or your family bring with you? You could list, in detail, the objects you find, or you could examine one object and write about it in detail.

2. Someone You Know: Think about the languages and literacies used by a family member or close friend. How do you know about this person's use of language, reading, and writing? When you enter this person's space (house, room, office), what literacy objects do you see? What has this person taught you about reading, writing, or even storytelling? Write a story about one moment you remember seeing this person talking or doing some sort of reading and writing.

3. Oral Stories: Think about the role of oral storytelling in your family or one of your communities. What kinds of stories are told? Who tells them? When are they told? Do these stories change over time, or change when different people tell them? Are they written down anywhere? Try to write about a specific story or storyteller in your family.

4. Exploring Your Community: Think about your home community or neighborhood. Are there any words, phrases, or sayings that are specific to this community? How would you explain these words to someone outside of this community? What are the speaking and/or writing practices of members of this community? Which people do the most speaking or writing?

languages and with different cultures. As part of this assignment, students could create language passports or licenses in which they document the languages they are learning in school and the languages they speak at home or in the community. Teachers could broaden this to include various online experiences as well: different computer coding languages, the languages used in video games, the languages of social media apps, and so on. Students can also record, perhaps in journals, their cross-cultural experiences throughout the school year, as part of writing prompts: "Things I notice about language and culture—in my school, in my community, at the grocery store, in the mall, at the airport, etc."

These kinds of writing opportunities, particularly when assigned in the early part of the school year, give teachers a window into the language profile, interests, values, and experiences that students bring with them to the classroom. Like the mapping activity mentioned earlier in this chapter, creating these writing opportunities for students can help teachers identify students' literacy strengths and interests (both in and outside of school) that can be tapped into or built on for future writing lessons and activities over the course of the year. Some teachers have also found that what they learn from multilingual students' literacy maps and identity texts help them develop points of entry for students into certain assignments, and can even be used to motivate students when they encounter obstacles in their work as writers.

Summary

In many ways, the "multilingual turn" is an aspect of English language arts teaching that we have embraced for many years. ELA teachers have long considered how we might add more multicultural perspectives into our teaching of literature, as we continually seek out novels, nonfiction, poetry, and authors that represent and bring diverse perspectives and stories to our students. We know that choosing culturally diverse and relevant readings can have a profound impact on the reading proficiency and engagement of our ELL and multilingual students. But ELA teachers also know that using multicultural literary texts can begin to build bridges between all their students and the worlds beyond their towns and borders. Stories and novels can and do bridge cultural gaps and create new understandings for students. There is even language in the CCSS that points to the benefits of more global perspectives in literacy standards and curricula. ELA Standard 7, for example, reads: "Students come to understand other perspectives and cultures."

But to date, we have not truly embraced this trend of multiculturalism and multilingualism in our teaching of writing. When it comes to writing, which is really about students producing texts for readers and audiences rather than reading and receiving texts, our discussions on diversity have been limited to ELLs and other students of culturally diverse backgrounds, often taking a "deficit model" approach. In this approach, teachers try to fill in students' presumed deficits—the missing pieces, so to speak—and bring ELLs "up to par" with their monolingual or native-English-speaking peers (Ortmeier-Hooper, 2008, 2013).

Even the global perspectives and aims of the CCSS are presented as a more receptive, even passive enterprise. For example, the language in ELA Standard 7 seems to suggest that most students in ELA classrooms will receive these experiences through reading and the consumption of literature, noting that students will "vicariously" inhabit these global and multicultural worlds. The standard does not consider a mainstream English classroom, where we already have many multilingual and culturally diverse students, like Ahmed, who don't just "vicariously" inhabit these worlds; they live in them and communicate in them daily. In the remaining chapters of this book, I illustrate how we can develop sound, research-based writing instruction, including assignment design, instructional methods, and response strategies, that are more inclusive and effective for all of our students.

Chapter Three

Inclusive Writing Assignments: (Re)Thinking Assignment Design

Notebooks as Artifacts

At the end of the school year, the students I've been working with leave me their English notebooks. As I thumb through the pages of white lined paper, I am struck by the sheer amount of writing in these worn, wire-bound notebooks. Dutifully kept by the students at the request of their teachers, these notebooks are artifacts of the students' day-to-day lives in their ELA classrooms. Each page meticulously displays the students' attentiveness to board notes and the teacher's directions on writing, new vocabulary, grammar lessons, and literary concepts such as plot and conflict. Each notebook carries with it the mark of its owner. Inside one are sketches and doodles of cars, skateboards, and the occasional portrait. The outer cover is scrawled with the student's handwriting and lyrics from his favorite rock band. Another notebook has the student's name on the cover in big, expressive letters with hearts and exclamation points. Inside, the margins of the lined paper reveal the inner life of her classroom moments, comments to friends written in Spanish, the occasional question in English, and the random heart or flower connected to the name of a love interest. In another, the cover ripped from the wire binding, notes about grammar and stories are interrupted by passages with drafts of song lyrics and half-written poems. Toward the front of the binder is a laminated English Grammar Tips handout purchased from the local bookstore. Each section of the notebook is labeled: grammar, literature, writing, and vocabulary. Notes are color-coded in various shades of red, green, blue, and black. Papers, including old tests with teacher's comments and grades, a short love note from a girlfriend, assignment sheets, and the occasional math homework sheet, are crammed in throughout the weathered pages.

Each student's notebook is in many ways a portrait of the student's individual social world and interests, a reflection of how the personal and the academic blur together in the contexts of middle and high school. Yet despite the different traits and talismans that inhabit these notebooks, they also share a commonality—they provide an intimate look into classroom experiences and the ways in which their owners respond to and consider the assignments their teacher assigns. Across many of these notebooks, the notes from class and the longer writing assignments exist as discrete and separate. In one notebook, the student copiously copied every word from the board in deliberate, careful handwriting, but he later admitted to me that he had no idea how to connect the notes to the writing assignment the teacher assigned afterward. Another student's notebook documents the teacher's assignments and then the student's numerous starts and stops, crossed-out sentences, and torn pages as she tried to complete a draft. From the teacher's vantage point, students' disconnections, confusion, and starts-and-stops often reveal themselves in other ways: short and underdeveloped essays, assignments that are never passed in or never finished, a more general lack of investment in writing.

Teachers hope that their assignments will engage and encourage students to write thoughtfully and even inspirationally. But as these notebooks demonstrate, too many students—especially ELL students—are not able to use those assignments to push themselves forward academically. The confusion highlighted in these notebooks might serve as a cautionary tale, leading us to ask how we can rethink our writing assignments to make them more inclusive and cognizant of the ELL and multilingual writers in our classes and more responsive to their needs. In this chapter, I focus on ways teachers might do this. I don't recommend a separate curriculum for ELL writers, but instead offer suggestions and frameworks to help teachers design writing assignments that can create more accessible, clear assignments that provide avenues of success for a wide range of student writers. I consider: How might teachers approach writing assignment design with ELL writers in mind? What factors contribute to assignments that don't work well for ELL students? What moves might help teachers create more successful assignments? And how might teachers sequence writing assignments across a semester or a school year in ways that allow students to build on their knowledge?

Why Assignment Design Matters

For ELL/multilingual writers, figuring out the assignment is often the first battle they encounter as they approach a writing task. Leki and Carson (1994) reported on a large survey of college-level ESL students and found that trying to understand and make sense of the teacher's assignment and expectations ranked in the top ten of their writing concerns. As English language arts classes become more diverse and teachers strive to have greater success with ELL/multilingual writers, the need for precision and clarity in writing assignments becomes crucial. ELL/multilingual students need more clarity, more background information, and more specific information about the teacher's expectations and goals (Raimes, 1985; Silva, 1993). They also need assignments that provide more clues about (1) how to find points of entry into the assignment, (2) how to see and engage with a writing situation as a social act, (3) how to generate language and feel more confident about drafting their ideas, and (4) how to build a repertoire of techniques and procedures that can help them develop more in-depth writing. Teachers will notice that many of the ideas I suggest in the following pages for best practices for ELL writers in mainstream ELA classrooms will benefit monolingual students as well.

Practical and Procedural Recommendations

Comprehensible Input and Assignment Sheets

When we think about practical and procedural recommendations, we might first consider how to make the assignments comprehensible for ELL/multilingual students (Echevarría, Vogt, & Short, 2010). Dana Ferris and John Hedgcock (2013), in their landmark book, *Teaching L2 Composition*, recommend that teachers provide clear and carefully constructed prompts for any given writing assignment. Each assignment should include an assignment sheet so that students have a tangible copy of what they need to do. Often when teachers write out assignments on the board, ELL students spend the bulk of their cognitive energy and time copying it down, and they miss out on some of the teacher's narrative commentary that may provide clues to the teacher's expectations. The assignments should also provide clear timetables and benchmarks for drafts, peer and teacher conferences, final drafts, and what students will need to hand in. Teachers should write assignment sheets with a balance between narrative explanation (Why are you writing this? What is the goal of this writing?, etc.) and easy-to-follow instructions that make assignment sheets more accessible to multilingual students. Bulleted points, timetables, check boxes, and benchmarks should all be part of the assignment sheet that students can refer to or bring to tutors who may be providing assistance at home or through additional tutorial support programs. Overall, assignment sheets should be clear, providing some sense of steps, discussions of topic possibilities, and a description of the presentation requirements.

Assignments and Procedures

Well-designed assignment sheets can be a powerful resource for students, particularly those who are often unsure how to unpack a given assignment to meet the teacher's expectations. I often revamp my assignments and my assignment sheets to make them more usable for students, based on their feedback.

If teachers are using classroom management systems such as Edline and Google Classroom, it is also helpful to provide step-by-step procedures for how students can upload and submit their work. Often these programs are difficult to navigate for students and parents. Teachers can also work with translators to provide copies of the instructions in the students' and parents' first language.

Length of Assignments

Teachers should also provide an expectation of length, but because our ELL students probably have varying English abilities, we might want to offer a range (e.g., three to six paragraphs, two to four pages, etc.). Given the difficulties students may have generating materials and the extra time many multilingual writers need, having a range in length requirement allows students to concentrate on the quality of their writing, not simply on the quantity.

Models and Assessment

Teachers should work very deliberately to deliver meaningful writing instruction, use models, and develop assessment tools that help to promote success for ELL/multilingual writers. Building a good assignment sheet without addressing writing instruction is not enough. In Chapters 4, 5, and 6, I explore specific ways of using models, feedback, and assessment tools to help multilingual writers become more successful in approaching writing assignments. The tips in these chapters will provide teachers with a stronger sense of how to build in benchmarks as well as assessment moments into the timetables for writing assignments.

The Importance of Context and Inclusivity

In addition to these practical considerations, teachers should consider context in their assignment design. Joy Reid and Barbara Kroll (1995) note that teachers designing writing prompts for inclusive classrooms should try to identify the contextual considerations that should shape the assignment and meet the needs of both teacher and students. They stress that effective writing assignments should:

- Be contextualized and authentic. Students should have a strong sense of the genre, the role of that genre in the world and how it is used by readers and writers, and how to connect a given writing assignment to their experiences in the classroom or outside of it.

- Be based on accessible content. Assignments should tap into the students' existing background knowledge so they can link old knowledge with new knowledge and experiences. Teachers might draw on clues from students' literacy maps (see pages 25–27) to think through the kinds of audiences, genres, and writing situations that might make an assignment more accessible and engaging for students. For example, a student who mentions the Boys and Girls Club as a literacy site outside of school may be more invested in writing about the ways such a club benefits area students or the broader community. Likewise, a student who shares that he reads Harry Potter in Chinese might be interested in writing about how the books or movies were reviewed and received in Shanghai or Taiwan newspapers compared to those in the United States.

- Be engaging. The tasks should involve students and should be of interest to both students and teachers.

- Be developed in tandem with appropriate evaluation criteria. (For a detailed discussion of evaluation and assessment, see Chapter 6.)

Concerns about Context and Building Background Connections

Flawed Assignments

How do these ideas play out in actual assignments? How might teachers develop assignments that lead to ELL/multilingual students producing their best work? Reid and Kroll (1995) offer readers a strong overview of what they call good quality assignments vs. flawed assignments, assignments that create difficulties for ELL writers and their teachers. Flawed assignments, they explain, are those that often leave ELL/multilingual writers at a loss as to where to begin or how to interpret the teacher's (and the genre's) expectations. In other words, these kinds of assignments can hinder the writing of ELLs before they even begin. Let's compare two flawed examples shared by Reid and Kroll.

From a science class:
Do a report on an astronomer who is currently living or has lived in the past 100 years. The report should consist of 4 or 5 typed pages and should be well written and well researched. (p. 274)

From a music class:
You will write a 3-5 page research paper on a musical topic. The purpose of this assignment is to familiarize you with music resources in the library. You must cite at least three different sources found in the library in your paper. This paper must be typed and double-spaced. The paper is worth a maximum of 60 points. It is due Nov. 6. (p. 273)

These first two assignments are not particularly ELL-friendly. The first, from the science class, lacks crucial information for student writers, particularly those writing in a second or third language. For one thing, it's not altogether clear what the teacher means by "report." Is this a biography? Is it an examination of the astronomer's scientific discoveries? Second, the assignment doesn't make connections to or extend the learning of the students in the classroom; there is no attempt to connect the prompt to students' background knowledge or previous experiences. In addition, it's not clear what the teacher means by "well written" or "well researched." In short, for the ELL writer, an assignment like this one offers very little to build on and can diminish the student's sense of purpose and confidence.

In the assignment from the music class, the purpose is made clearer to students, and it provides more information about how they might use sources, including basic information about where they can obtain them: the library. We also know what the paper is worth in terms of points. The genre ("research paper") may also be clearer to students—if they have had experience with the genre in the past. But if students are unfamiliar with the genre, then the purpose, expectations, and objectives of this assignment are hazy. The content, "a musical topic," also is vague. ELL writers will have little idea how they might find a viable, researchable subject, one that will work for the assignment in terms of scope, interests, quality, and time. The assignment also gives no clue about audience, which students need in order to consider the impact of vocabulary choices, tone, and even how to shape the genre. Is this a research essay that might appear in a magazine like *Rolling Stone*? Or *Vibe*? Or *Latin Beat*? Or is it a report that might appear as a Wikipedia or encyclopedia entry?

The Problem with Decontextualized Assignments

In many ways, the preceding assignments represent what might be called "decontextualized" or "low-context" writing assignments. They give students very few clues about the kind of writing that is expected (the genre), who might be reading it (the audience), and how the text might be used by the reader (the purpose). There is also no clue about how students should view or understand their relationship to the audience. In other words, these prompts have very little to no context that can help a reader get started and figure out how to appropriately perform the task. The prompts are not envisioning writing as a socially situated exchange between reader and writer. They are lacking in what I've come to term *rhetorical fingerholds* (Ortmeier-Hooper, 2013).

What Are "Rhetorical Fingerholds"?

In rock climbing, climbers use fingerholds to move themselves vertically and even horizontally in order to climb higher. Climbers can often scout out potential fingerholds from the bottom before they start, and even while scaling the rock face they are continually scanning for crevices in the rock they can grab on to and then use that fingerhold to help their bodies move to new angles and new positions on the rock. Mastering each fingerhold is a success, and eventually, by the strength of those holds and their positioning on the rock face, climbers can move toward the top and completion. When we write, we have similar fingerholds: rhetorical ones.

Rhetorical fingerholds—clues about audience, the writer's position and relationships, the genre, the purpose and subject—are important keys that help us to develop contextualized or "high-context" writing assignments for student writers. High-context writing assignments are more accessible to linguistically and culturally diverse students, in part because they make the act of writing a more communicative one. ELL/multilingual writers often have a great deal of experience in negotiating across cultures and languages. They have often had years of experience in responding and adjusting to different audiences through oral speech and home languages. When we create "high-context" writing assignments, we provide students with opportunities to build on those communicative skills and harness them for their writing.

Here is an example of a high-context assignment that offers these kinds of rhetorical fingerholds:

> Produce an informative three-fold brochure *[length, genre]* explaining *[purpose]* to the public *[audience]* why they should or should not support the building of a new children's museum or new library *[subject]* in our neighborhood *[writer's position = a member of the neighborhood]*.

In this example, the following rhetorical fingerholds provide students with some starting points for how they might want to shape and write this piece:

> Fingerhold #1: *Genre (and length): an informational three-fold brochure.* Students can find and study examples of these kinds of brochures in order to think more critically about how they might use and need to adjust tone, language choices, headings, visuals, and other characteristics in their own texts.

> Fingerhold #2: *Writer's purpose and position: a member of the neighborhood.* Students understand and can develop better understandings of their communities and neighborhoods. They may already have a strong sense of the stakeholders in this discussion, including friends and family, and that in turn creates opportunities for adolescent writers to draw on those relationships and narratives to provide strong details and examples.

Fingerhold #3: *Audience: the public in the student's town or city*. Students may not know everything about the "greater public" of their city or town, but they do know the neighborhoods and some of the issues from family members and also from being residents themselves. Teachers can also help students build their knowledge of their city or town for an assignment like this one so that they are able to appeal to that audience. For some novice writers, the teacher might even adjust the audience by narrowing it to an individual or set of individuals (the mayor or city council, for example) to make the prompt more accessible and visible.

Fingerhold #4: *Subject: new children's museum or library*. Here again, teachers can adjust the subject to make it more accessible to the students in the classroom. The idea of a library might appeal to students who are interested in a library's free community services, such as computer and Internet access, book collection, book club, or place to hold local events. Students with younger siblings or relatives may see the value of a children's museum, especially if they have had a chance to visit one in the past. This prompt could just as easily consider the addition of a new school auditorium or soccer field. In any of these cases, students can locate a point of entry into writing the brochure that is connected to some aspect of their personal lives and interests.

How Rhetorical Fingerholds Create Flexibility

Each of these fingerholds presents students with an accessible set of circumstances that reflects an authentic aspect of a writing situation. Each set creates opportunities for them to think critically about and even discuss how they as writers might approach their craft, their goals, and their words. Writing assignments like these help students move from seeing writing as a passive task, only done to get a passing grade in the teacher's gradebook or on the test, to seeing writing as an engaging and purposeful thinking activity.

To connect students more strongly to that sense of purpose, teachers can consider the kinds of roles student writers may already be playing in their homes, their workplaces, their schools, or their communities. Over time, teachers can also use these rhetorical fingerholds to help stretch their ELL/multilingual students' perspectives, sense of agency, and aspirations for the future. For example, they can embed writer's roles in these prompts that encourage students to consider roles they need or want to play in their schools, in potential workplaces, as small business owners, as professionals, as future politicians, as future parents, as college students. The goal is to use the fingerholds in a writing prompt to help writers stretch personally and academically and build in some creative thinking about what they see as possible.

The same kind of adjustments can be made to focus on audiences, subjects, or genres. For writers who struggle, teachers might begin with subjects that students

Introducing the Academic Language of Writing and Rhetoric

Though I always talk about "fingerholds" with students when we talk about their work as writers and as we approach new writing situations and assignments, I also look for opportunities to introduce them to academic language. In the classroom, this means that I share definitions for words (such as *genre, audience, purpose, conventions, argument, essay, prose, synthesis,* and so on) that are a regular part of developing an academic writing vocabulary. As students become more comfortable with their roles and tasks as real writers, I make a point to start using the academic language tied to a particular outcome more regularly, and I encourage them to do the same. We always come back to the comfortable metaphor of fingerholds, and it remains a concept that I find particularly useful when I develop writing projects and write prompts for students. At the same time, I believe that helping ELL/multilingual students develop and feel comfortable using the more official terminology of writing and rhetoric is part of preparing students to be successful academically. For many of them, the official terminology makes them feel like they are gaining access to a privileged discourse, and I want them to feel entitled and empowered to use that vocabulary in my classroom and beyond it.

are already familiar with (e.g., current interests, personal experiences, etc.) and then move toward subjects they are less familiar with but that they can pursue through home and/or community resources that have knowledge of the subject. More advanced writers might respond to prompts that ask them to consider subjects that are less familiar and require additional reading and research. The same is true for genres. Teachers can begin with genres that students see in their daily lives (informational brochures, newsletters, news stories, narratives, etc.) and then help them advance to genres that may be less familiar (e.g., arguments, political position papers, researched essays, workplace genres).

In the Classroom

An Argumentative Literary Assignment

In Mrs. Keller's[2] class of mostly multilingual writers, the writing prompt for an argument assignment was built in response to the students' reading of *The Scarlet Letter*. After reading the book and the screenplay and watching a film version of the novel, students were ready to tackle an argumentative essay. Building on their knowledge of the novel and the Puritan time period that had been covered in class, Mrs. Keller developed the following writing prompt:

> You are a community member in the Puritan village. In fact, you are a lawyer, and your job is to convince the community who is the greatest sinner in the story of *The Scarlet Letter:* Hester Prynne, Rev. Arthur Dimmesdale, or Roger Chillingworth. Write an argumentative speech (two to four pages in length, double-spaced) that you will give at the town square. Support your argument to the com-

munity with examples from the book (which may include summaries of specific scenes, descriptions quoted from the novel, or quotations from the characters).

> First drafts will be due Nov. 1.
> Peer Review will be on Nov. 5.
> Intermediate Drafts will be due on Nov. 9.
> Final Drafts will be due on Nov. 12.

During class discussion, students in Mrs. Keller's class, most of whom were ELL and bilingual writers, were able to identify the rhetorical fingerholds in this prompt:

- Puritan community member and lawyer (writer's role)

- Convince the community that Dimmesdale/ Prynne/Chillingworth is the greatest sinner (purpose and subject)

- Town square/Puritan, religious community of adult men and women (venue and audience)

- Write an argumentative speech (genre)

Mrs. Keller helped students talk through how these fingerholds might impact their texts and their decisions as writers. The specific method Mrs. Keller used is outlined in detail in Chapter 4. But in general, this high-context prompt enabled less confident ELL writers to develop ideas more fluidly and to bring playfulness and voice to a style of writing that had been difficult for them in the past. The prompt also created good opportunities for Mrs. Keller to help students develop strategies for adding length and depth to their writing because she invited ELL students to draw on their oral strengths, as well as their critical thinking strengths, to share their viewpoints on the social dynamics of this writing situation.

Student writers could talk through ideas about how to approach the argument and possibilities for reaching particular members of the audience because they had a very clear sense of the task. For example, when Lidia seemed to stall in her writing and complained that she had nothing else to say, Mrs. Keller asked her what kind of argument might be particularly persuasive to the Puritan women in the town. Lidia, writing as a lawyer trying to condemn Dimmesdale, noted that women might be persuaded if she wrote more about the young child, Pearl, who was an innocent in the middle of this affair, and about the ways in which Dimmesdale had abandoned his child. Suddenly Lidia could see the possibilities for a new paragraph and a new angle to her argument.

On Your Own

Think of a current writing assignment that you regularly teach. How might you reshape the assignment to provide students with clearer benchmarks, a stronger sense of context, and better "rhetorical fingerholds"?

Are there ways that you connect an assignment and writer's purpose to familiar situations in the students' communities or make connections to other kinds of writing that they've already experienced, seen, or written in another context? Consider how Mrs. Keller connected Lidia's comment about telenovelas (see next page) to draw her further into her goals and purpose as a writer for the *Scarlet Letter* assignment.

As she started writing, she told Mrs. Keller that *The Scarlet Letter* reminded her of a telenovela, and that she was going to try to write in a dramatic fashion that might be even more appealing to the female listeners in the crowd. The high-context prompt created opportunities for these kinds of exchanges and gave Mrs. Keller's writers a tangible sense of how writing might work in a situation like this one.

In the Classroom

An Exploratory Essay on Gender Roles

Reid and Kroll (1995) provide another example of a high-context prompt from a more upper-level English course. In the original assignment, students were asked to write an expository essay exploring gender roles by considering how their lives might change if they had to live as a person of another gender for two weeks. In the following adaptation, students are asked to explore ageism and social roles by considering how their lives might change if they had to live as a senior citizen or middle-aged parent for two weeks. They were asked to draw on personal reflection, memories, observations, analysis of their observations, culture or country traditions, and gender roles, and employ critical thinking skills to consider the scenario from multiple angles. This is an assignment that was given a few months into the school year, when the teacher felt that a sense of community and trust had been established among the students.

Age and Social Roles (adapted from Reid & Kroll, 1995, p. 265–66)

Imagine that you have two weeks to live as a person of another age: as a senior citizen or as a middle-aged person. That is, if you are a teenager now, imagine that you will live for two weeks as 68-year-old retiree OR imagine that you will live for two weeks as a 40-year-old parent. Think of the difference in social roles, everyday life, and feelings you might have. Use some of the questions below to begin your prewriting:

A. What about your life would be better? Try to list at least three things.

B. What about your life would be worse? Try to list at least three things.

C. What about your life would not be changed? Try to list at least three things.

D. How would your gender and your culture (or the country where you were living) impact your choices and your life at this age? Try to list three things.

E. What would you enjoy most being able to do in those two weeks that you can't do now? Describe one thing in detail.

F. What would you least enjoy having to do in those two weeks that you would probably have to do? Describe one thing in detail.

Write a two- to three-page (typewritten, double-spaced) essay in which you discuss how age and perspectives about age can impact the lives and social roles of people, using your prewriting and personal observations to support your opinions. Your audience will be a classmate with whom you will discuss your idea and who will review your essay drafts with you. You will also share your ideas and your final essay with a reader representing the age group you have chosen to examine. Your final draft (and all preliminary drafts) is due November 14.

Your essay will be graded on the following criteria:

- Organization

- Content

- Mechanics

The age/social role assignment featured (1) simple and clear directions, (2) a scenario to consider as students wrote, (3) a fully articulated audience ("a classmate" and "a reader representing the age group you have chosen to write about"), (4) length requirements, (5) easily located purpose ("essay in which you discuss how age and perspectives about age impact the lives and social roles of people, using your prewriting and personal observations to support your opinions"), and (6) a clear sense of the sources to draw on for the content of the essay: personal reflection, memories, observations, and analysis of these experiences. All of these sources were readily accessible to students, and ELL/multilingual students could also draw on a range of personal observations, including culturally informed ones from their home communities and countries, if they chose. The teacher provided guiding questions for prewriting with specific recommendations ("Try to list at least three things.") in order to provide students with starting points. These questions also offered a possible organization structure, and the teacher complemented the assignment with in-class discussions about organizational possibilities in the expository essay genre, as well as discussions about how students could integrate evidence into their writing. Peer review and teacher feedback after the first draft were also part of the assignment design.

Questions to Consider for Creating More Inclusive Writing Assignments

- What is the reason and purpose for the writing assignment?

- Who are the students who will complete the writing assignment and what are their needs?

- How does the assignment fit into the immediate classroom curriculum and ongoing lessons? How does it fit with overall course objectives?

- How is the content of the prompt accessible to ELL and multilingual students? Do students know all the terms, or will I need to gloss some of them?

- Can I provide a range for page expectations and length? [Given that length is often more difficult and time-consuming to produce when writing in a second language.]

- How will the content of the prompt engage students in considering authentic or socially situated writing events? How will it engage students by connecting the content of the prompt to authentic, real-world situations or ongoing classroom literary or research content?

- Have I included clear rhetorical fingerholds that provide students with a sense of the writing situation they are addressing?

- How can a writing process (multiple drafts, peer review, teacher response, self-assessment) be built into the assignment design to engage the students and help them internalize their growing knowledge and skills as writers?

- What knowledge, language and communicative abilities, and critical thinking skills should ELL/multilingual students have opportunities to demonstrate in the writing process? And in the final written product?

Teachers may also find it useful to refer to English language development standards, like those created by the WIDA Consortium (https://www.wida.us/standards/eld.aspx), for more ideas on how to adapt lessons to the various language levels in a given classroom.

Considering Cultural Bias in Writing Assignments

Even the most exciting assignments that teachers create to engage their students can prove to be challenging for some ELL/multilingual writers, especially assignments that assume students have been educated in the United States: a prompt on the rap music of Kendrick Lamar; the importance of the Superbowl; late night television; the Beatles and the British Invasion; Rosa Parks and the protests in Birmingham, Alabama, in the 1960s; slavery in the United States; the Civil War, etc. For some multilingual students, particularly those who have been in US schools for years, these kinds of references and prompts won't be an issue, because they may have studied or heard of them in other contexts. But for others, more recent immigrants and arrivals, these kinds of writing prompts are embedded with popular culture and an assumption about prior education they may not have. The result is that ELL/multilingual students can feel removed and disengaged from assignments and the classroom in general.

Given the ways in which writing is already seen as difficult and treacherous terrain for many second language students, writing assignments that seem impossible or inaccessible can lead the most vulnerable ELL students to give up academically. This is particularly true if they feel they have no way to be successful.

Many students will be reluctant to admit this to their teachers because in doing so, they will have "outed" themselves as different, as outsiders, and feel that such admission only amplifies the way a teacher might see them as less capable or less intelligent than their monolingual, native-English-speaking peers. Given this issue of mistrust and doubt, teachers must think critically and reflectively about how their assignments position students. Teachers have to consider how they may be inadvertently embedding cultural bias into their assignments in ways that push ELL/multilingual students to the margins of their classrooms.

Consider the following prompt asking students to analyze advertisements in their daily lives:

> Advertisements reveal a great deal about a society's assumptions about values, desires, and self-image. Choose a television ad currently running and write a critical analysis, using the following questions to guide your analysis: Who is the target audience? How do you know? What does the ad assume about the audience? What is the ad's main message? How do you know? What messages are embedded in the ad? How do you know? What kinds of visuals or music (or other sounds) are used? What do these visual and audio cues contribute to the direct and indirect messages? Overall, what does this ad tell you about the cultural context of the advertisement?

Why is this prompt problematic from a cultural standpoint? First, the assignment assumes that students have access to TV programs or the Internet (to watch shows online). Some students may have social and financial constraints—i.e., lack of a TV or other technology, or access to these devices, in the household—that make this prompt difficult. Furthermore, we know that today's students, regardless of their language backgrounds, are viewing fewer conventional TV programs. Instead, they are watching TV without commercials through streaming and Netflix, watching home language TV shows via YouTube, watching international soap operas from South Korea or India with English subtitles, or viewing programs on cable channels such as HBO, Univision, and Telemundo.

This prompt, then, assumes a singular, monolingual TV audience, when the reality is that students today have a much stronger sense of how diverse the viewing audience really is. In some ways, these possibilities make this assignment more exciting and potentially engaging. But to open up those possibilities, the teacher will need to address some of that diversity in the prompt and perhaps explicitly suggest that students consider looking at commercials that appear alongside their Google searches and on their smartphones, and commercials they can view in their home languages or those aimed at members of their home countries and communities. Many ELL/multilingual students will assume that commercials in languages other than English aren't even an option here. Often, ELL students assume that the English teacher cares only about English and that the English classroom does not allow for non-English perspectives or examples. The teacher will need to make the non-English advertisement a formal option and encourage students to see it as a viable, challenging, and interesting choice. During class time, the teacher might use some non-English examples or ads from other English-speaking countries so that all students have a sense of how ads are targeted to different consumers (audiences) around the world. Many of these are readily available through YouTube and other video sites.

Moving beyond Graphic Organizers and the One-Shot Writing Assignment

Thinking about Writing in Terms of Writing Projects

> Independent, extended writing is really the goal of the L2 writing class, for while writers do not learn to write *only* by writing, they cannot learn to write without writing.
>
> —Ken Hyland (2003, p. 132)

How many writing assignments should teachers implement in a school year? This is a question I often hear from teachers. I ask teachers who work with linguistically diverse classrooms to think through how to provide their students with the most meaningful writing experiences, not only in terms of personal value, but also in terms of craft and critical thinking. Sometimes teachers and students are more successful when writing assignments are extended and embedded in larger meaningful activities, and not just tacked on to the latest reading or grammar lesson.

Developing Multiple Aims for Writing Projects

The kinds of writing projects that provide the most opportunities for ELL/multilingual writers to advance their skills as critical thinkers and writers should include multiple aims. As Johns (1999) suggests, these kinds of writing projects should:

1. Draw on student knowledge of genres and social situations, and then help to apply that knowledge to analysis and critique of known and new texts.

2. Continually create opportunities for students to adjust and revise their ideas of genre. Ultimately the goal should be to move them beyond homogeneous forms like the five-paragraph essay and other formulaic writing.

3. Provide opportunities for students to assess, expand, and revise their strategies for approaching a writing task so that they can develop new strategies and ways of thinking that will help them respond to a wide array of writing tasks and situations, both in school and out of school.

4. Develop students' abilities to research different kinds of texts, experiment with a variety of writer's roles, and experience various kinds of contexts and writing situations.

5. Cultivate a metalanguage for writing. ELL and multilingual students can—through self-reflection, self-assessment, and classroom dialogue—develop a more explicit understanding of how they as individual writers, readers, and critical thinkers can respond to, analyze, and figure out texts and textual expectations.

(adapted from Johns, 1999)

The problem with the decontextualized approach to assignment design is that the important critical thinking and engagement opportunities that can occur and help student writers to develop a stronger sense of investment and craft get lost.

Ann M. Johns (2011), a second language writing specialist, argues that teachers who think beyond the prompt and more in terms of an extended writing project have the advantage of building a more critically engaged and socio-literate writing classroom. When teachers design these kinds of writing projects, students are doing more than simply linking vocabulary and verbs on the written page; they are building an understanding that all texts are social: "important written and spoken discourses are situated within specific contexts and read by individuals whose values reflect those of the communities to which they belong" (p. 291).

Extended writing projects include not only the task and the procedure, but also opportunities for reflection and research built into the timeline. For some assignments, like the *Scarlet Letter* example, this time for research and reflection included discussions about characters as well as how students might use textual evidence to support this particular writing task. They also had time to brainstorm and consider counterarguments through informal in-class journal prompts that later became material students could draw on to add more depth to their final drafts. In other words, the writing assignment was not simply handed out to students with the expectation that they would complete it in a day or two without any more input or discussion from the teacher or classmates. The assignment was the start of classroom activities and discussions that illustrated the habits and decisions of writers. The writing project also included drafting and revision as well as teacher and peer feedback. Even the assessment of the final product asked students to write a reflective cover letter and self-assessment, in addition to the teacher's assessment. The assignment was conceived from start to finish as an involved project, rather than a one-shot essay completed over a three-day span.

In many ways, embedding a writing prompt in an extended writing project allows students to move past some of their limited, constricted ideas of what a school genre looks like, or the robotic approaches they may employ in an effort to just "get it done." Presenting writing assignments as extended projects can provide teachers and students with a chance to analyze and "value the genres of their first cultures, to approach all texts as socially situated, and to reflect on their experience with text processing" (Johns, 2011, p. 293). In doing so, ELL/multilingual writers internalize more ideas and strategies about how to write, and they develop more advanced and more confident writing skills for the future.

The Power of Sequencing Writing Assignments

The Problem of "Always Starting Over"

The question of time required for reading and writing in a second language places many ELL/multilingual writers in a situation where they are continually playing catch-up with the assignment and other members of the class. Students who still struggle with reading and vocabulary are often unable to "marshall information on a topic, analyze it, and synthesize it" as quickly as they may need to for a writing assignment (Leki, 1992a, p. 19). The cost is that students in this predicament often don't have time to develop their writing and are continually dealing with a "Sisyphus moment" in their writing skills (Ortmeier-Hooper, 2013). Just as these young writers have a stronger sense of their ideas, are ready to pay attention to revision, and are ready to build a stronger draft, the assignment is due. The rock of writing they have diligently been pushing up the hill rolls back down, and they have to start all over again. As Leki notes, "the crux of the problem may lie less in the subjects that students are asked to write about than in the structure of traditional writing classes. . . . [I]n a typical writing class, the teacher assigns a topic, suggests a range of topics, and then establishes a deadline date for the final draft" (p. 19). Even if the teacher takes a multidraft approach, there is an end date, "a certain point the assignment is considered finished and students move on to a new topic unrelated to the previous one" (p. 19).

Teachers often don't anticipate at the outset of an assignment that some student writers will have difficulties. After all, papers are being written and graded.

Progressing across Assignments: Looking Back in Order to Jump Forward

How can teachers organize writing projects to provide ELL and multilingual writers with a clear sense of progression across assignments? While there is no one right way to do this, a good start is to explicitly discuss the links between assignments with the class. When introducing a new writing assignment, particularly a new genre, teachers might begin by asking students to recall the traits they discovered and learned about in the previous assignment. What worked for them as writers during that assignment, and what difficulties did they encounter? For example, I often teach the genre of personal narrative after the research paper, which can feel like quite a leap to my students. So in class, I ask them to consider moments when research-based writing may have included aspects of narrative writing or storytelling. They point to feature stories on famous celebrities, or news stories on current events from magazines and blogs they follow. We talk about how personal writing can often serve as a "hook" for research and other more traditional academic genres by letting readers know about the writer's personal investment in the subject or by sharing how another person's life was impacted by the subject at hand. We talk about how personal essays, and narrative writing more generally, can resonate with readers and why. This leads us into discussions on the characteristics of strong narrative writing and the purpose of narrative when shared with readers. In these ways, we begin to forge links across genres, and I show them the ways in which even academic genres, such as research writing, informational writing, and arguments, are infused with aspects of narrative, and that narrative writing can also be infused with research, analysis, interviews, and observations.

But teachers eventually start to notice diminishing returns. Multilingual students do not seem to make much progress as writers, particularly in developing their drafts, enhancing their vocabulary usage or sentence structures, or adding more detail or length to their final products. At the end of the school year, students have generated a series of papers on a number of topics, but their writing development may not have progressed as much as the teacher or student had hoped. These students have no sense of mastery over anything they have produced. From the students' perspective, they keep trying to master the vocabulary of one topic, only to have it replaced by the vocabulary of a new subject in the next essay.

Building a Sequence

To counter this lack of progress in writing development, Leki (1992a) proposes that teachers consider sequencing writing assignments so that the topic of one paper leads to the topic and the refinement of that topic in the next assignment. Leki writes, "[T]he work done for each assignment serves as the basis for the next assignment, building students' skills (including vocabulary and educating since the same terms and structures are likely to appear in subsequent papers)" (19).

Here is how she describes one such sequence:

- The first assignment focused on students' current knowledge. Students selected a subject, wrote about what they already knew about the subject, including the significance of the subject in a community or society, and then addressed how they were personally invested in the subject. Students had to demonstrate a strong personal connection to the subject in order to continue.

- The second assignment, a summary essay, asked students to find three pieces of publicly available information about the subject. Students could use pamphlets, online articles, government documents, and even films and documentaries they had seen. Students then summarized the three pieces in an essay format, introducing readers to the subject and contextualizing the sources.

- In the third assignment, a survey assignment, students created and distributed a survey to at least twenty people about their subject and its impact on the community. Students had to write and design the survey, which was reviewed by peers and the teacher. Once they had distributed and collected their surveys, students learned to use the data to write a report about their findings.

- A subsequent interview assignment required students to interview an expert. Experts could include professionals involved with the subject or individuals in the community who were impacted by the subject. Leki had students develop interview questions and then record and take notes during the interview. They then synthesized excerpts from the interview into an overview of what they had learned.

On Your Own

Think about the current writing assignments that you give. What are some ways you might sequence the writing assignments in your course? How might sequencing writing assignments help students make connections and pull from their developing knowledge of a given topic and its vocabulary across assignments? In developing a strong sense of sequence across assignments and genres, you can allow students to build on current themes or topics and help them have a stronger sense of ownership over vocabulary and those topics. This strategy also helps student writers to establish more concrete links across the genres and their topics.

What might students learn about writing from observing how a topic can shift or take on new dimensions in different genres and for different audiences?

• The fifth and final writing assignment was a longer persuasive, researched essay that had students bring together elements from the first four assignments. In this final essay, students drew on the earlier papers to write a new essay infused with students' "authorial expertise" about their subjects, with the aim of convincing readers to become stakeholders in the subject.

Leki's approach has been implemented and further developed by many ELL teachers in a variety of settings. In all cases, the goal is to help students establish a sense of authorial expertise not just in their subject matter but also in their writing. Since the students often revisit certain vocabulary and concepts across the five papers, they are able to offload some of their cognitive concerns about vocabulary as they delve into each assignment. Leki and others have observed that this gives students more time and energy to dedicate to their craft as writers, attending to issues of organization, making more effective decisions about how to use their writing to affect readers, and showing an enhanced willingness to revise across drafts, particularly in the final assignment.

When subjects and writing assignments are disconnected in ELA classes, many students attribute the shifts to changes in subject matter or to the teacher's idiosyncrasies. The sequencing approach helps student to realize, think through, and compare the ways in which genre, audience, and purpose can alter a writer's approach. Other teachers, drawing on Leki's approach, have used a three-essay sequence in which students move from

        personal narrative →

            researched essay/informational text →

                argumentative essay.

A student might, for example, write about his experiences in a refugee camp in Jordan, and then follow up with an informational text on the education made available to refugees in these camps or a research-based pamphlet for fellow students on how the United Nations vets refugees. This might be followed by an argumentative essay for the local paper outlining the ways in which becoming a sanctuary city for refugees has benefits for the broader community. All of the writing projects are tied to the same subject matter but targeted toward different audiences, some with different purposes, and all employing different genres. The movement across the projects helps ELL and less experienced writers see how subjects, writing styles, writing conventions, tone, and even language choices can shift across genres and audiences.

Missing Pieces in Assignment Alignment and Assessment: How We Sometimes Overlook the Gap of Instruction

Often when I go to teacher conferences that consider ELL writers, numerous discussions focus on ways to help students become stronger writers. Experts offer interesting and provocative approaches to designing assignments, and teachers share creative innovations and student work derived from those assignments. Inevitably, though, the conversation dives into issues of alignment and assessment.

Some sessions focus solely on assignment design, discussing many of the strategies and concerns I address in this chapter. Along those lines, presenters and experts show complex algorithms and graphics that demonstrate how certain assignments have been aligned to a whole host of standards. Over the years, these have included TESOL standards, NCTE-IRA standards, individual state standards, ESL consortium standards, and, more recently, the Common Core State Standards. The efforts to align curricula are important, and I have been involved in a number of school- and state-based alignment initiatives over the past two decades. These alignments can help teachers think through their curricula in systematic ways, making sure that beloved assignments are also meeting student needs and objectives for their development.

The second iteration of these conversations focuses on formative and summative assessments that should be attached to assignments. Again, these assessment conversations are tightly tied to conversations about standards and alignments. I see these conversations as being two ends of a spectrum, but they often miss the integral pieces in the middle about actual instruction and classroom teaching practices (see Figure 3.1). Alignment and assessment are worthy conversations to be having, but we also need to be paying more attention to how teachers implement assignments and develop better practices for actual writing instruction in diverse classrooms. We can certainly align our curricula in ways that reflect the skills our ESL students should be learning and mastering. We can also chart their progress to identify the gaps and the skills they are still learning or need to learn. We can share rubrics, testing prompts, evaluation scales, student scores, and so on. The problem with these conversations, however, is that none of them deals explicitly with the teaching of writing and the writers themselves.

Figure 3.1. Noticing the instructional gap between assignment and assessment.

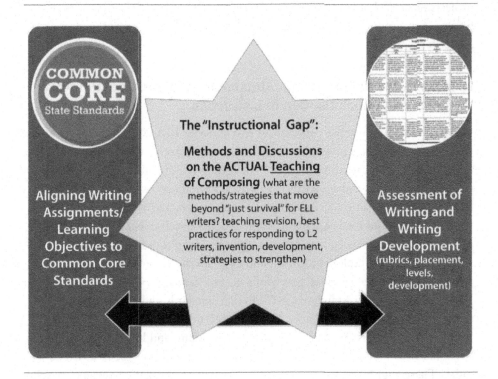

The reality is that many of the mainstream methods of teaching writing that have become the staple of our ELA classrooms were developed without considering multilingual students. Frequently these methods have been normed on the experiences and successes of monolingual native-English-speaking students. Even as new textbooks and writing programs emerge with notes about ELLs in the introductory passages, or those little text boxes that make suggestions on adaptations for multilingual students, they do not offer a method of teaching writing or set of instructional practices that have been normed on the more diverse classrooms that ELA teachers are encountering. The next two chapters begin to address that gap by considering instructional methods of teaching writing to ELL and multilingual writers in mainstream ELA classrooms. After all, how we teach writing to this demographic addresses the very real and practical concerns of teachers who work with these students in their classrooms on a daily basis.

Teaching Writing Explicitly: Methods for Writing Instruction in Mixed Classrooms

"I don't know how to write."

Bishnu, a sixteen-year-old student from Nepal, tells me that she doesn't write much in her English language arts class. It is a lower-level academic track, and though they do a great deal of reading, she hasn't ever really felt like a writer. I ask her about the written work she does do, and she tells me that she writes many single-word, single-sentence, and sometimes single-paragraph answers to questions about the readings. "No one has ever really asked me to write or taught me how." She assumes that she isn't asked to write much because English is her second language, and she confesses that she doesn't really mind that she is never asked to write. Avoiding writing is something she prefers. She worries that her English writing will be embarrassing, and confesses that she just isn't good at it.

Bishnu's experiences aren't particularly unusual or new. In 2004 the National Commission on Writing noted that the amount of time dedicated to writing in most schools was often inadequate. Teaching writing takes time, as does responding to student papers, and teachers often feel that there are too many other curricular goals to pursue and too little time. As a result, teaching writing in an explicit way is often shortchanged, and our most vulnerable writers, especially ELL/multilingual students, don't often complain.

In this chapter, I share concrete examples and suggestions for making writing instruction a much more hands-on and engaging classroom event for English language learners and monolingual English speakers in ELA classes. This approach is increasingly gaining resonance in writing and TESOL studies because it builds on students' background knowledge and scaffolds meaningful instruction.

Using Genre Approaches to Writing

The genre-based approach at the heart of this chapter stems from research on systemic functional linguistics (SFL). SFL was originally developed by literacy and education scholars in Australia (e.g., Christie & Derewianka, 2008; Derewianka & Jones, 2013). Whenever I mention systemic functional linguistics in my teacher education courses, the terminology creates varying degrees of suspicion and a few panicked looks. Systemic. Functional. Linguistics. It doesn't sound like an approach that would be readily accessible to students. It also can be a bit off-putting for many ELA teachers who worry that their strengths as English teachers do not reside in linguistics training. But SFL approaches, as they are commonly called, have a great deal to offer ELA teachers, and the approach has some parallels to other rhetoric-based approaches as well as process-based approaches that many teachers will find familiar.

For example, SFL approaches consider how rhetorical situations, writers' intent, purpose, genre, and tone are all important considerations for novice writers. SFL approaches also encompass a process approach that helps students think through how writers revise and improve on their writing across multiple drafts. In recent years, the approach has been refined and developed further by scholars working with ELL writers in US schools (Brisk, 2015; de Oliveira, 2013; Schleppegrell, 2004; Schleppegrell & Go, 2007).

Although aspects of SFL will seem familiar to many ELA teachers, it is important to note that SFL uses a distinct and deliberate set of practices, cycles, and oral opportunities that create important points of access for bilingual and ELL writers, who are sometimes on the margins of our writing classrooms. These deliberate points of access provide teachers with a better window into the "funds of knowledge" and competencies that ELL/multilingual students can bring to the critical thinking aspects of writing (Moll, Saez & Dorwin, 2001). Recent longitudinal studies have documented that the SFL method has led to stronger student writing, more confidence, higher test scores, and more active engagement in the ELA classroom (Brisk, 2015). One of the reasons I am dedicating an entire chapter to this approach is that it offers some concrete strategies for actually teaching these concepts and others (such as revision, writing with detail, and sentence structures) to our student writers. It's also a technique that provides students with opportunities to bring their oral proficiencies and knowledge of language negotiation into the writing class.

What Is SFL?

Simply put, an SFL approach leads students through a step-by-step process in which they study a genre by first analyzing how model texts are constructed (known as "joint deconstruction"), take what they've learned about the genre and collaboratively create a text (known as "joint construction"), and then build on that

---

The Terminology of SFL

In examining the social context and functional aspects of a text, SFL scholars use the following terms to help students and teachers understand these contexts, or the "register of a given text," with more precision:

- *Field:* What is happening, what are the dynamics of the social interactions taking place in the text; what exactly are the readers and writer engaged in, and how does the language they use play a role in this interaction?

- *Tenor:* Who are the readers and the writer taking part in this interaction? What do we know about the social roles and the relationships between readers and the writer? What might we need to know about the status and power roles between the readers and the writer?

- *Mode:* How is the text organized? What rhetorical modes (persuasive, expository, didactic, etc.) are being used? What is the "channel of communication, such as spoken/written" used by the writer (Halliday, 1985, p. 12)?

For some students, explicitly learning about these terms can be helpful for analysis. For others, the terms can be too far removed from the texts they encounter daily or the texts they themselves are trying to write.

In the pages ahead, I outline examples of how teachers can use an SFL approach with their students, drawing on classroom examples and research. Some examples and discussions use the SFL terminology, explicitly pointing to *field, tenor,* and *mode.* Others draw on the concepts but provide ways to help pull students into this kind of analysis without what the more reluctant or less confident student writers may see as a roadblock of terminology. In the end, I am always cautious about inadvertently creating roadblocks or obstacles for reluctant ELL/ multilingual adolescent writers because they prevent such students from feeling like they understand or that they have much to contribute to the conversation. These roadblocks undermine students' willingness to take chances and prevent them from gaining more confidence in their writing. However, I also acknowledge that for more mature, more advanced writers and users of language, teachers should not shy away from experimenting with "upping" the language used around conceptual frameworks like SFL and encouraging students to feel a sense of ownership of the more technical, academic terms.

experience to create their own text (known as "independent construction"). Along the way, teachers and students focus on the rhetorical situation that leads to the creation of a text—noting audience, purpose, situation, and genre—as well as the moves that authors make to have an impact, from tone or voice to word choices to grammatical concepts. Commonly, SFL encourages teachers and students to work through and analyze the context of a given text and its author's intent, as well as the goals and conventions of the genre. In other words, the method encourages writers to consider the social situation or context and the functional aspects of language at play in a given text.

As I walk through aspects of this approach, writing teachers will see similarities to their current methods of instruction. However, they will also notice that an SFL approach has four specific qualities: (1) a focus on the rhetorical situation; (2) extended talk time dedicated to writing practices and decisions; (3) emphasis on tangible materials and what I call "Big Paper" moments; and (4) recursivity and embedded teaching and learning cycles. In addition, the method highlights the need for and use of collaborative analysis and collaborative writing, along with active in-class modeling by both students and teacher, to build student confidence, their writing repertoires, and their authority as real writers and readers of English. Together, these qualities lead to more active involvement of ELL/ multilingual writers in mainstream language arts classrooms. Here's how.

Focus on the Rhetorical Situation

The SFL approach considers how rhetorical situations—writers' intent, purpose, genre, and tone—are concepts that help writers get words onto the page and shape them into appropriate, even compelling texts for readers. The approach emphasizes discussion, textual analysis, and writing situations in which students and teacher openly consider the writing task at hand. These discussions are the springboard to the student writer's own text, and as such, they commonly help students begin to see writing as dynamic and communicative, as opposed to flat and stagnant. Teachers work with students to see how a writer can set the context and to understand the field within a given genre or for a particular writing task. The SFL approach also unpacks and makes the concept of "genre" more varied, socially embedded, and useful to young writers.

Stretching Concepts of Genre

Historically, English teachers have identified genre in terms of literary genres: poetry, narrative, memoir, essay, play, short story, novel, novella, and so on. But as we began to consider the role of informational and professional texts in our daily lives, the concept of genre has stretched beyond the literary and beyond the fiction/nonfiction binary that librarians often use to describe their libraries to young readers. Our discussions of genre now include texts such as recipes, lab reports, scientific articles, op-ed pieces in a newspaper, feature stories, résumés, proposals, research essays, movie scripts, print ads, BuzzFeed columns and surveys, eulogies, cover letters, business correspondence, grants, and more. The truth is that these days, we and our students encounter print and writing everywhere. Each of these genres is socially situated, reflective of a certain intent on the part of the writer, and directed toward a certain audience.

The Common Core State Standards emphasize three specific types of texts at the secondary level: argument, informational, and narrative. As de Oliveira (2013) has cautioned, "The emphasis on informational writing raises specific linguistic challenges for ELLs. Many ELLs do not have experiences with informational texts in their home lives and, therefore, may be unfamiliar with the language expectations of informational texts in school" (p. 41). In addition, scholars have long proved that the argument traditions taught as "normal" or "standard" in US educational contexts are culturally influenced and may not be the norm in other languages and countries.

ELA teachers should consider that ELL and multilingual students may have little contact with these "standard" kinds of writing, making it more difficult for them to achieve the same kinds of success as their monolingual classmates. The SFL approach builds on ELL students' strengths, oral capabilities, interactive and hands-on instruction, and students' inherent knowledge of language use as a communicative act in order to create more buy-in from ELL students, who often feel as though they are at a disadvantage when it comes to writing in English.

Extended Classroom Discussion

One important aspect of the SFL approach is that it explicitly brings a higher level of discourse and classroom discussion into how we teach writing in the ELA classroom. For many ELL and multilingual writers, oral language skills may be much stronger than written language skills. Even if they have higher-level writing skills, some students may have more confidence in sharing their ideas orally than in sharing their reading or writing in English. In addition, many ELL/multilingual writers have a strong experiential understanding of how language use shifts across various stakeholders and audiences, often from years of negotiating across multiple languages, generations, and communities in their daily lives. In other words, they may have more to say in conversations that consider how a given text is used in society and how the writer uses language to anticipate and respond to readers. SFL helps students to establish a better sense of their strengths and to build on those strengths, even if they still struggle with putting words on the page. The approach also allows for many hands-on opportunities for individual students, the teacher, and the class as a whole to engage with the text in tangible ways—which makes writing a less passive activity, one that isn't just about finding the right answer in the book and copying it down.

Tangible Materials and Big Paper Moments

One material condition that is noticeable across the many studies of SFL is the teacher's use of a projector (and/or Smart Board), large butcher-block paper copies of printed text, and the whiteboard or chalkboard. The large paper/visual aspect of the approach—in which texts, by both professionals and students, are publicly displayed as large visuals so that sentences can be read and analyzed by those sitting far and near—instills the sense that writing is socially situated and shared by communities, that discussions about writing can be had. This Big Paper approach creates moments for teachers to demonstrate certain behaviors about revision, commenting, and even reading that can help students when they work on their own or in their other classes. Another noticeable feature is that teachers have opportunities to cede their place at the front of the classroom and let students interact with (write on, manipulate, revise, comment on) these large visuals of texts.

In my own experiences with the SFL approach, the decision to cut corners with this aspect of the teaching leads to less interaction, less understanding, less critical thinking about writing, and a less attentive classroom of student writers. In short, the materials used in this method matter. Profoundly so.

Here's why.

The Big Paper part of this approach signifies to students that writing is not a passive activity—and a text is rarely finished without input or reaction from readers. Students are always a bit surprised to see their writing exhibited in such a large fashion. As one student noted, "I've never seen my writing so big before. It's huge. It actually looks like something. You can actually write on it, see how you can move things around." The large exhibition of texts helps to establish the idea that our writing is a tangible tool that we use and manipulate to make work, not just an artistic endeavor that only a few can master. The Big Paper or projection of texts also creates classroom artifacts that teachers can come back to at different phases in the SFL cycle; for example, an artifact from a joint construction can be used to talk about revision ideas or recommendations when students become stalled during their own individual constructions and revisions. For teachers the visual classroom artifact reinforces the idea that writing (and writing well) takes effort, requires critical thinking, involves discussion, and is a hands-on, active pursuit. In other words, it requires both students and teachers to go all in.

Recursivity and a Teaching-Learning Cycle

As Luciana de Oliveira (2013) has noted, SFL approaches stress a cyclical method to writing instruction, often returning to the same model texts throughout the unit to illustrate writers' decisions at the sentence level, the genre level, and the global level. Once students master the vocabulary and meaning of a model text, they get to return to it to decipher and analyze more discrete elements of the writer's text. The cyclical nature of this process also provides students with a sense of familiarity and authority in discussions about a text.

For many ELL readers, the imposition of too many model texts can distance students from the task at hand. They may spend more time reading the text than writing about it. If there are too many texts or if texts aren't well chosen, ELL/ multilingual students spend much more time than their monolingual peers wrestling with vocabulary and comprehension, leaving little time to contemplate the writing (how the text came into existence, writer's choices, how it persuades or captures readers' attention) or to develop the critical analytical skills needed to talk about writing. A cyclical method that consistently comes back to a few models allows ELL students to become master readers of those texts, contributing to classroom conversations and collaborative writing activities (see Figure 4.1).

Figure 4.1. Teaching writing with the SFL approach.

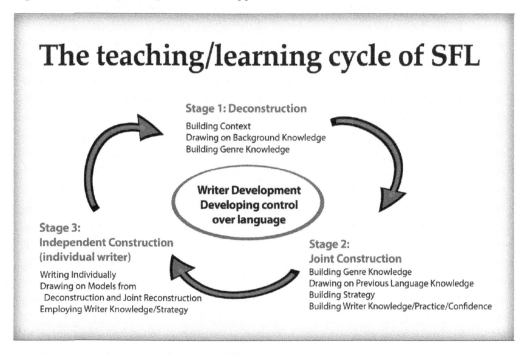

Incorporating Translanguaging Perspectives

An SFL approach is not necessarily at odds with the dispositions that translanguaging research encourages for teachers and students. In fact, the open classroom discussions about how writers use all their language resources to negotiate their meaning and intentions with readers is aligned with the translanguaging perspective. Teachers using an SFL approach can encourage students to draw on first language (L1) strengths and experiences in class discussions and in their writing.

The cycle includes three major instructional components that can be adapted to any major genre or writing assignment: deconstruction, joint construction, and individual construction. Extensive opportunities to explicitly teach revision and language use are embedded in the joint construction and individual construction components of the method. De Oliveira, Klassen and Maune (2015) define these components as follows:

1. Joint deconstruction—the whole class works together to analyze a text in order to build a sense of context and field.

2. Joint construction—the whole class collaborates to write a text.

3. Individual construction—individual students craft their own texts.

Within each of these components, SFL offers concrete strategies for explicitly teaching these concepts and others (such as revision, writing with detail, and sentence structures). The method is adaptable to a number of genres, and in many ways an SFL approach creates a pattern of instruction that can settle the anxieties of more cautious or less-experienced writers. Once students become familiar with the pattern, the use of a similar teaching method across genres allows teachers to broaden their expectations and encourage ELL writers to pursue more complicated writing and rhetorical situations as the year unfolds.

In the following sections, I walk through the various steps of this cycle, demonstrating moments for recursivity, providing some sample talking points for group discussion, and illustrating the SFL approach with excerpts from the classroom.

Stage 1. Joint Deconstruction of the Text: Reading as Writers

Analysis of a Writer's Intent/Stance/Genre/Audience

Many great books about teaching writing discuss using and showing models to student writers. Penny Kittle (2008), for example, points to model texts as an important way to introduce students to new genres. For teachers who work with ELL/multilingual students, however, it is often not enough to hand out a sample mentor text. Even reading the text aloud in class may not provide the opportunity for students to engage with the text as writers or provide them with an opportunity to analyze it. They are often unsure about what to look for in a text or how to analyze one in ways that help them get a stronger sense of the writing task at hand. The SFL approach builds on the idea of using model texts, but it takes a more hands-on, culturally responsive, and discussion-based approach to models and exemplars. I like to think of it as "active modeling," or *text deconstruction* (the SFL term).

Thinking about How Texts Work

In the teaching of literature and story, English teachers often analyze, or "break down," the novels and short stories we share with students. We introduce concepts such as figurative language, symbols, plot, conflict (man vs. man, man vs. self, etc.), character development, and setting. These concepts serve as a framework for how we want students to talk and write about their readings in class and on paper (see Figure 4.2).

In an SFL approach, the teacher and the students work together to break down—analyze—texts. But the goals and concepts—even the questions teachers ask—are introduced to help students understand how texts work and the kinds of choices writers make and why they might make them. But before that conversation can get started, the teacher's first priority is to find the right models.

Figure 4.2 Classroom board demonstrating the deconstruction of a text through teacher and student input.

Choosing Appropriate and Culturally Responsive Models

Choosing text models is often the most time-consuming yet essential part of SFL writing instruction. Finding the right texts—ones that are culturally accessible, allow for teachable moments, and have the potential to engage student interest—is a tricky challenge. To demonstrate some of the thought process behind text selection, let me share some experiences from the classroom. Here I'll delve into details on choosing texts for a personal essay in both a narrative unit and an argument unit.

For Mrs. Keller's class, we began the narrative unit by looking through examples of flash nonfiction. One of our criteria was that the stories had to have relevance or interests across cultural boundaries. We also wanted pieces of a length that students could easily read in the time allotted. Mrs. Keller had taught narrative writing in the past using Amy Tan's "Mother Tongue" as a model text. In many ways, Tan's piece was a great choice, but it had led to some difficulties as a model for writing. Although the piece was culturally accessible and interesting, Mrs. Keller found that it was too long—almost ten pages. The length led to three issues: (1) it took a long time for students to read and understand the details (which meant that reading the text dominated the unit—taking more than a week of close reading and discussion), and thus instructional time for student writing and a focus on students developing their own craft as writers was shortchanged (only three to four days); (2) it was difficult to explore all of Tan's wonderful writerly moves throughout the text; there were just too many, and that led to a diminished focus on examining the text from a writer's perspective; and (3) the students could not imagine writing a ten-page narrative themselves, nor did they have the time.

So when Mrs. Keller began using the SFL approach, her first task was to find models that could work for the purpose of teaching writing and that were still literary and engaging to her teenage students. She found that flash nonfiction held the answer. In the sidebars here and on pages 65–68, I share in more detail the rationale behind our decision and the discussion that led us to settle on two specific models. As you can see from that discussion, it's important for teachers to think through the rationale guiding their text selection with their ELL/multilingual writers in mind.

Finding Flash Nonfiction

Here are some excellent sources for locating short "flash" nonfiction texts that work well for deconstruction activities on essays, narratives, and even arguments. Unlike excerpts from longer short stories, book chapters, or memoirs, flash nonfiction offers teachers and students stand-alone pieces that provide a complete narrative within a succinct scene or moment.

Brevity: A Journal of Concise Literary Nonfiction: http://brevitymag.com/

Kitchen, Judith, & Mary Paumier Jones (Eds.). *In Brief: Short Takes on the Personal.* New York: Norton, 1999.

Kitchen, Judith, & Mary Paumier Jones (Eds.) *In Short: A Collection of Brief Creative Nonfiction.* New York: Norton, 1996.

Narrative Unit: Choosing Models from Creative Flash Nonfiction

"The Deck" by Yusef Komunyakaa

In "The Deck," the author writes about using his father's tool—a hammer—to build a deck for his home. The essay provides wonderful use of detail and action to describe the building of the deck. At the same time, he makes connections to family, inheritance, and what we carry on from our fathers and mothers, as well as a concrete connection to a tool that has been passed down from one generation to the next.

What we liked about the piece:

- We could easily develop quickwrites and journal prompts based on the story that might lead students to their own narratives. For example, after reading the text, we asked students to write in their journals about an object they had used or that had been given to them by a relative (grandparents, parent, aunt, uncle, etc.). The object could be a tool (like the author's hammer) or a piece of jewelry or clothing, or even a kitchen tool. The prompt was actually used three times in freewriting activities. In the first one, we asked students to describe the object in detail, trying to use three out of five senses. In the second, we asked them to describe in detail the person who had given them the object. In the third, we asked them to write about a memory of that person or a time when they had used that object. These quickwrites eventually became foundational texts for students' joint construction.

- Reading this two-page (about seven paragraphs) nonfiction text was an achievable goal for all students (it is also published as a prose poem). Its length meant we could read it in class, and we could return to it multiple times to discuss certain features, sentence structures, and language choices.

- The text included examples of varying sentence lengths, sensory detail, reflection, and even dialogue.

- The reading was culturally accessible. Though not every student could relate to building a deck on their home (some of our students lived in apartments without decks), they could all relate to the idea of building or making something that had a connection or a memory tied to a family member or a person in their lives. For recent immigrant students, these memories and tools could be tied to experiences in the United States, but they could also be tied to memories of and tools they had in their homelands.

- The story was accessible to students as teenagers. Each student in the room could relate to the writer's position (being a son or daughter), and the ways in which one might try to make sense of or honor a relationship with a parent, guardian, or grandparent.

continued on next page

"Missing" by Celine Geary

An evocative piece of creative nonfiction about the author's relationship with her grandparents.

Why we liked the piece:

- We could easily develop quickwrites and journal prompts based on the story that might lead students to their own narratives.

- Reading this two-page (about five paragraphs) nonfiction text was an achievable goal for all students. Its length meant we could read it in class, and we could return to it multiple times to discuss certain features, sentence structures, and language choices.

- The text included examples of varying sentence lengths, sensory detail, reflection, and even dialogue. It had a compelling lead as an introduction and a striking ending. It also experimented with questions and one-word sentences, both of which were used as devices to engage readers.

- The story was culturally accessible. The narrative focus on the author's concerns about how her grandfather and grandmother would react to her actions resonated for students. They all could relate to the idea of trying to meet the expectations (and dealing with disappointment) of parents, guardians, grandparents, and other adults in their lives.

- The reading was surprising and also accessible to teenagers. The nonfiction narrative focuses on the writer's memory of being a teenager. She reveals that she had a child out of wedlock and was fearful of being shunned by her grandparents. Mrs. Keller and I knew that the "having a child out of wedlock" piece of the narrative would be somewhat edgy for the students. But we also knew that the real-life aspects of the reading would heighten students' interest. In addition, we knew that some students in the room had relatives and friends who were already young mothers.

Argument Unit: Choosing Models from Publications, News Websites, and Op-Ed Printed Sources

For the argument unit, we chose sample student texts from previous classes, but we also chose texts by published writers. In this case, we found argumentative essays from the *New York Times* and other news sources with strong editorial sections. The argument unit followed the reading of Hawthorne's *The Scarlet Letter*. We wanted to find a piece that showcased a strong argument essay; we also wanted it to be topical. The first model text, an op-ed from a reporter's blog on the stoning of a woman in Afghanistan for adultery, provided a twenty-first-century connection to the story of Hester Prynne.

The second model text, from the *New York Times*, was also topical—an argument on students' overuse of earbuds and the rise in hearing problems among youth. It connected to students' day-to-day concerns and activities.

Both models:

- Were accessible in length.

- Were engaging and connected to current events or problems. They also provided opportunities for interesting discussions about the topic, not just the writing.

- Were written for a real purpose and what students saw as a "real audience," not just for a test or from a textbook. The teacher spoke explicitly about where the texts originated: the *New York Times* and the openDemocracy website.

- Included particular aspects of the argument genre: counterargument, claim, evidence, and appeals. The pieces contained clear examples of transitions and illustrated how to use secondary sources in ways that complemented the writer's voice and that were integrated. In addition, the pieces used certain rhetorical devices to engage readers (questions, dramatic use of sources/statistics, opening narratives, examples, etc.).

- Were accessible to teenagers. The blog about stoning and adultery captivated students because its content was charged with issues of sex, women and men's behaviors, relationships, and crime and punishment. The article, "An Argument against Headphones," was less politically charged but still of interest, particularly given students' habits. Many entered class each day with earbuds in, and the teacher often had to remind students to put them away during class time. They were interested in the science presented in the argument, but it also was a piece that students felt they could take a position on. The reading led to excellent arguments in the classroom over the wearing and not wearing of earbuds, and these in turn created wonderful opportunities for the teacher to present writing lessons on fallacies, counterarguments, a writer's use of statistics and sources, persuading the audience, and author credibility.

continued on next page

Lesson Learned:

We also used a few examples from the students' ELA textbook, but we found that students lost interest the moment we said, "Open your textbook to page 97." Suddenly the promise of writing like real writers vanished, and the idea of writing was reduced to a school-based activity. Even real-life articles that were published in textbooks felt stale, rote, and too school-like to the students. To counter that resistance, we paired textbook readings with examples from real-life publications and sources. When we came in with a printout or clipping from newspapers or journals, the students were intrigued. We also found that clippings and printouts allowed us as a class to write in the margins, circle sentences and parts of sentences, and create a more visceral, hands-on experience with reading and deconstructing the texts and the authors' writerly moves.

Choosing Model Texts: Criteria Checkbox

- ❐ Teenager-friendly

- ❐ Provocative

- ❐ Themes that connected to the students in the room (grandparents, familial ties and tensions, relationship issues, universality)

- ❐ Engaging language use

- ❐ Authentic (For many of our students, this meant that the sample texts were **not** from a textbook—even a good textbook!)

- ❐ Short and achievable in length

- ❐ Writing/language skills we wanted students to learn = *clear link between our objectives for them as writers and the model texts*

Examples from the narrative unit:

- ♦ Pieces that used dialogue

- ♦ Variety of sentence and paragraph length

- ♦ "Showing, not telling" for narrative and argument essays

- ♦ Strong use of detail, flashbacks, quotations, etc.

- ♦ Strong sense of writer presence and voice

Resources for choosing texts:

- ♦ Flash nonfiction

- ♦ The Learning Network at the *New York Times.*

Getting Started: Deconstructing for Social Context and the Roles of Reader and Writer

Once text models have been chosen, teachers are ready to introduce students to the deconstruction phase of the teaching-learning cycle. As I mentioned earlier, with SFL approaches, teachers and students work together to analyze the model texts. This activity is similar to literary analysis, but again, the goals and concepts—the questions that teachers ask—are introduced to help student writers realize how texts work: to see the craft that goes into developing a certain feeling in readers, to consider the kinds of choices writers make, and to explore how those decisions show up on the written page.

The focus of class discussion during deconstruction, therefore, is on how texts work in social situations, or how they facilitate certain responses and actions on the part of readers. Teachers begin by talking about a text's function and purpose in society, while at the same time encouraging students to look closely at how the writer constructs the text. The goal here is a discussion that includes both teacher and students. In the sidebar on page 70, I share some sample questions that can be used during deconstruction so that teachers get a sense of this kind of discussion and have some model questions to help guide them in their own classrooms with their own students.

Teachers will find, however, that they need to help guide student talk in order to help students look more closely at the text from a writer's viewpoint (see the sidebar on this page for a sample of this kind of "guided talk"). In some ways, teachers can start guided talk by sharing and demonstrating the kinds of questions they ask as readers and writers when they look at a text. But the key is to pass the baton to students and encourage them to start talking as readers and writers themselves. Teachers might also use journal prompts to encourage students to write about specific features they notice within the text or about how the text develops writing and readability.

It is important for teachers to try to complete deconstruction with at least two different but similar exemplar texts. The first text deconstruction is teacher guided with discussions and collaborative documents; the second deconstruction is guided with more student input, using student partner pairs and responses. In general, I have found that it can take students a few tries to become familiar with analyzing writing in this way. They aren't used to thinking about the social situations

A Sample of Guided Talk

In deconstruction, the teacher always has a "writerly" agenda, not necessarily a literary one, as seen in this excerpt from a discussion about a nonfiction essay:

Student: I think the author feels sad.

Teacher: Okay, good point. But how do you know that? **What** does she write, **how** does she write, how does she use certain words, sentences, phrases, even punctuation to make you feel that? Let's look more closely at the writing. Tell me what you see.

Sample Questions to Guide the Deconstruction Discussion

- Why/How do you think we might use this sort of text in our society?

- What could we call it?

- Where might you see or read a text like this? Have you seen one before? Where? Why did you read it?

- So why do writers write this kind of text? *[purpose]*

- Remember when we were writing explanations *[arguments, blogs, etc.—refer to any past writing assignment]*. Why is this text different from an explanation? How so?

- Look at the beginning of the text. What do you think the writer is doing here? What does the beginning tell the reader?

- What name could we give to this sort of beginning? What about a term like *orientation* to remind us that it's setting a scene?

- Which words link up the text and show us when the action took place? We could call these "linking words."

—Questions adapted and excerpted from Derewianka (1990, pp. 5–6).

Additional question specific to the sample nonfiction text "Missing":

- What is the relationship between the narrator and the grandparents in "Missing"? Which phrases, images, details, and sentences show that to you as a reader? How do details and dialogue help us as readers to understand?

Additional questions for a second day of deconstruction:

- Identify the **short sentences** in the story "Missing." Why do you think the author chose to write these short sentences? What do they show you in the story?

- Identify examples of **longer sentences** in the story "Missing." Why did you pick these sentences? What do they show you in the story? *[Teacher can place these on the board to examine in further detail.]*

- Identify an example of **dialogue** in the story "Missing." How is it punctuated? Why is this important? What effect does it have on how the reader understands the characters or the story?

- Identify and write out the sentences in the **present tense** in the story "Missing," and then write the sentence before and after it. What do these show you?

that guide writing and/or certain genres. They aren't always used to thinking about how language helps writers to achieve certain goals. But as students, as both individuals and as a classroom community, become more practiced in these types of discussion and analysis, they are able to "take apart" texts with far more independence and confidence. As this happens, students' voices begin to take a greater role in leading the discussion, becoming more authoritative as students feel like "real" writers themselves. Occasionally, teachers will find that new genres or more high-stakes writing tasks will stifle that confidence, and everyone will feel as though they're starting over. But with encouragement from their teacher, student writers often quickly realize that the analytical skills they have developed will help them learn and develop new strategies for even the more daunting writing tasks.

In the Classroom

A Sample Deconstruction

Mrs. Keller and her students read the first sample text, a brief memoir, of a unit on nonfiction essays and narrative. In this first step of deconstruction, she reads aloud while students follow along with a copy of the text at their desks. As a second step, Mrs. Keller leads the students, ninth and tenth graders in a mixed classroom, through a guided talk about the writer's choices and the way this kind of text works in society and for readers.

Teacher: Why do people write these narratives or memoirs?

Student: To write about the most memorable moment in their life!

Student: To give information or advice for another person's life.

Student: So they can show others their feelings.

Student: People write memoirs to tell people more about their past life. What was it like in the past and how you could survive it?

Teacher: Where do we find these stories in society?

Student: When we talk about or to honor dead people.

Teacher: Yes, sometime we use personal stories in eulogies—these are the speeches we give at a memorial service or funeral.

Student: We find these stories in blogs and on Facebook, etc.

Student: We find these stories by teachers showing us people's work and writing.

Student: Everyone in a society has stories like this.

Student: Sometimes in magazines.

Teacher: Yes, sometimes these are essays or feature stories. How do people use these stories in society?

Student: People use these stories to tell other people what happened in their past.

Student: It shows others how they struggled.

Teacher: I like your use of the word *show* here. It does feel like we can "see" her story here. We are going to talk about how we can write to "show" readers our experiences. Other ideas of how people use . . .

Student: People write memoirs because it's easier to tell a story; it doesn't have to be long.

Teacher: True, this one isn't long. Some memoirs are entire books and much longer. Other ideas?

Student: They use these stories to express their opinion.

Student: They use them to boost their self-esteem, to feel like something mattered.

Teacher: What do you think this particular writer's purpose is? Why is she writing this?

Student: She's writing because she is missing her grandpa.

Student: To give us ideas and to let us think about our life and sometimes it reflects our feelings.

Student: The purpose of this story is to tell people about the most memorable time of her life.

Student: It is meant for people who have experienced the same fate and can relate.

Student: Her audience is us [teenagers], because she writes about being a teenager.

Student: Her audience is everyone; people who like stories.

Student: I think she wrote it for her family and the supportive people in her life.

In the second day of deconstruction, Mrs. Keller encourages students to talk about more textual features in the model text. In this case of narrative writing, her objectives include some of the following:

- How to write with both sensory and specific details; the difference between "showing" and "telling"

- Varying sentence structures

- Using dialogue to move a narrative forward

- Writing openings/leads (how to grab the attention of readers)

- Transitions

- Time management and pace in narrative writing (chronological time, flashbacks, compressing time, etc.)

- Use of past or present tense (discussed through attention to the writer's use of flashbacks and current-day reflection)

- Use of imagery, metaphor, and symbols/objects of meaning

In deconstruction, students are encouraged to see written texts as social, communicative, and often a negotiation between the writer and his or her audience. Deconstruction discussions are framed by the teacher's continual emphasis on how the author connects with his or her readers, the decisions the writer has made, and how certain features can create reactions and connections for readers. Focal features are identified in the model texts and discussed using collaborative Google documents, student notes and turn-taking at the whiteboard, whole-class discussion, and prompted journal responses. In this classroom, Mrs. Keller encourages mandatory participation by distributing popsicle sticks. Each student gets one or two popsicle sticks, and each time they participate in the classroom activity and discussion, they pass in a stick to her and collect participation credits.[3] These acts of participation are added in to their formative assessment grades for the unit.

Teachers can also return to deconstruction later in the unit for specific lessons on structure, punctuation, and language usage. Brisk (2015), for example, encourages elementary school teachers to return to the model texts to discuss changes in verb tense or transitions from one section of prose to the next. Similarly, Mrs. Keller returned to deconstruction at a later point in her argument and narrative units (during the joint construction phase) to reemphasize and help students consider what makes for a powerful ending, how to use repetition or alliteration, how to punctuate dialogue, and how to heighten their use of symbols and metaphors.

Deconstructing for Academic Language

Deconstruction also offers opportunities for teachers to help students build a stronger understanding of academic discourse. In doing so, teachers can draw students' attention to language features and writerly choices that can help them elevate their sentences, the cohesion in their topics, their word choices, and the details of their written texts.

Luciana de Oliveira (2013) uses deconstruction to help students develop more precise and strategic understandings of textual meaning. She describes textual meaning as a way of analyzing texts for thematic choices, thematic development over the course of an essay, and lexical cohesion. In her classroom, she worked with students to examine two sample essays for an assessment exam, one deemed high-scoring and one low-scoring. She and the students then studied organizational patterns from the higher-scoring essay in order to understand what scorers/readers valued about that particular text. For both essays, they tracked themes (particularly in the form of nouns, pronouns, and noun phrases) to list out what was being discussed (and the words used to discuss it) over the course of the essay. This analysis was done at the sentence and paragraph levels. The class then compared the two lists side by side.

Students noticed that the writer of the stronger essay used more specific language, including more precise nouns, nouns that provided readers with details and sensory cues. The writer of the lower-scoring essay employed more pronouns and used more basic vocabulary choices for his nouns and verbs. Students also noticed that the writer of the stronger essay employed academic language or vocabulary from the writing prompt and from specific subject areas. The higher-scoring writer used pronouns only in a very deliberate fashion to achieve a certain effect, often to avoid repetition or to link previous concepts and nouns. De Oliveira also had students examine connectors (e.g., "therefore, "as a result," "however") and discussed how these function. With the teacher's guided talk, students began to see how connectors helped readers recognize how ideas related to one another. Students identified places where the writer used connectors at the beginning of sentences or paragraphs to show relationships between ideas that had already been discussed and new ideas about to be introduced. One outcome of this kind of comparative analysis was that students could see that high-scoring essays were not a mystical, magical, unachievable object. Instead, students began to understand that writers can make purposeful language choices, often through revision, that lead to a stronger, more effective text for readers.

When Deconstruction Goes Off Course

For mixed classrooms with ELL students, ELA teachers may find that they need to facilitate deconstruction and encourage conversation. Many ELL students are used to working strictly on graphic organizers and often alone when writing. These practices tend to be limiting and less challenging, but there is comfort in the routines too. The oral aspects of the SFL writing approach mean that teachers can continually check for comprehension and clarify concepts. For example, when Mrs. Keller introduced the narrative sample "The Deck" by Yusef Komunyakaa, all students were able to identify the setting and main characters. ELL students in the room also pointed to the author's use of short fragments and one-word sentences for effect. But when it came to the point of the narrative's primary symbol, the hammer, some ELL students articulated very little understanding of the tool and its use as a literary device. As Ali noted, "It got the job done." Students like Ali didn't comprehend the literary function of the hammer as a talisman for a particular memory and person of importance to the author and its inclusion as a device to create meaning. And since the students had completed the deconstruction for homework and outside of the class discussion, they missed out on this important point. Understandably, then, when Mrs. Keller had students write about a tool or object in their own lives that held meaning, Ali took the prompt quite literally and wrote four paragraphs about a tool, a screwdriver he had used the previous week-end to fix a door. The paragraphs were informational, with very little description and almost no narration. Though he had read and deconstructed the model text on his own and completed the homework, Ali had not picked up on the memoir genre's goals of connecting a special object to a specific memory or person. He had missed the purpose of the writing assignment, and Mrs. Keller had not been able to address this misunderstanding because the homework assignment had not yet been graded. When he realized that he had misunderstood the model and the assignment, Ali was embarrassed and even more reluctant to share his writing with others. In his eyes, the experience confirmed his belief that he was a bad reader and writer in English.

It is vital to keep the deconstruction cycle as a classroom activity because it helps to create multiple opportunities for understanding, questions, and explanations. The whole-class dialogue allows teachers to gracefully troubleshoot these kinds of concerns and also to openly praise the contributions of ELL writers. During deconstruction conversations, teachers can also let students have short check-ins with partners to help less confident students vet their questions before throwing those questions and ideas out to the broader class.

Stage 2. Joint Construction: A Turning Point That Moves Students from Readers to Writers

Writing is a risky activity. For ELL writers, this is particularly true, and studies over the years have shown that ELL/multilingual students often pull away to try to avoid writing. The fear of writing with error, a sense that they lack the right word—all of these fuel a lack of confidence. Joint construction, the next part of the SFL instructional cycle, creates a situation in which unconfident writers can build cconfidence, skills, and strategies for their work as writers. In joint construction, the teacher and students build a text together as a class, an activity that can help students demonstrate oral, rhetorical, and writing competencies, and one that also allows teachers to see the contributions and insights of ELL/multilingual writers. Many teachers working with ELL writers voice the concern that they don't see progress on the written page, but students are often developing as writers of English in ways that are not obvious on the page. Joint construction helps teachers identify these strengths, which often manifest in a discussion as the group composes the class text. These insights provide teachers with more knowledge about the building blocks that ELL writers can be encouraged to turn to and draw upon when they write.

Developing a Shared Topic

Joint construction begins with the class working together to understand and articulate the goals of the writing assignment and the genre. Many ELL writers struggle with understanding writing tasks and assignments. Indeed, even at the college level with monolingual native English speakers, instructors often find that students don't spend enough time reading and thinking through the objectives of an assignment. So joint construction begins with the lesson that understanding the objectives and expectations of a teacher's assignment is not always an easy task. Teachers can point out clues and demonstrate how students can decode a given assignment, its objectives, and the expected procedures so that they can recognize the academic language of certain tasks and interpret teacher expectations more confidently.

The teacher then leads students to decide on a topic they all have an interest in and can contribute to. For a narrative assignment, it can be useful to think through the events or places students have in common. For example, is there a common school event, a community experience, an adolescent reality or experience that all students have some familiarity with? In one classroom I worked with, the sophomores had all had the experience of failing a test or exam, and they decided to write about that. In a junior class, students were concerned with driver's licenses, and they all had some common experiences with learning to drive. In a third class, the one I share in more detail below, the students decided to write a narrative about an especially harsh winter in New Hampshire, where twelve-foot piles of snow had interrupted traffic, parking, and even work within the city. The snow, creeping up ever higher on sidewalks and corners around the city, had captured students' attention. It was the highest accumulation of snow on record, and everyone—from teachers to students to parents to bus drivers—was impacted by it. The students also knew the assignment called for a great deal of description, and many of them had compelling facts and personal stories to share. They quickly told their teacher that writing about the winter conditions would be a good match for the narrative assignment.

Discussing Audience

Constructing a text as a class also allows for conversations about audience. As a group, with teacher guidance, students begin to use vocabulary and concepts (purpose, situation, the use of a text) gained from deconstructing a model. The teacher can interrogate certain ideas, asking students to dig deeper and refine their concepts of audience even further. In the construction of the winter narrative, for example, students began by suggesting that parents, grandparents, and fellow New Hampshire residents would be the readers for the piece. But Mario, a student from Honduras, disagreed. He argued that it wouldn't be very interesting to people who were living in New Hampshire because they already knew what the streets covered in snow looked like. Other students began to agree with Mario's point, and one suggested they should write for people who did not experience snow and only saw the stories about New England's winter on the news. Again, consensus emerged, and the teacher began to write the potential audience on the board (see Figures 4.3 and 4.4).

> Audience: fellow teenagers from more southern states who had complained about a few inches of snow.

> Purpose: to share a vivid portrait of how "real" amounts of snow had impacted the students in New Hampshire.

Joint construction is most effective and garners the best kinds of interaction when the topic emerges from the students themselves. Students should have a sense of a real audience that might be interested in or affected by the text.

Figure 4.3. Developing a joint construction: Deciding on a topic and an audience.

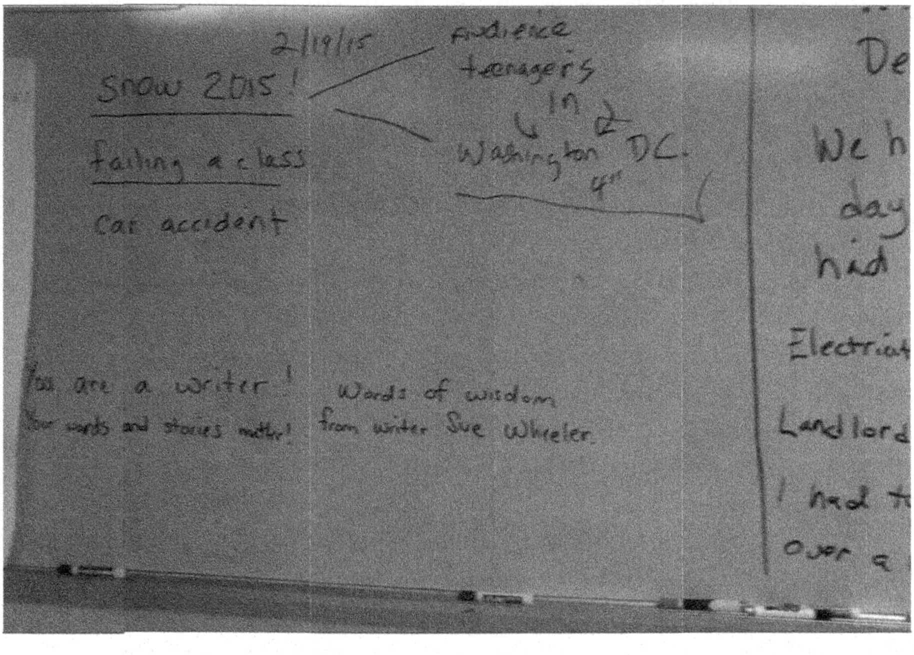

Figure 4.4. Developing a joint construction: Building the narrative as a class--winter in New Hampshire.

Volunteering Ideas and Sentences: Building Writing Stamina

After students and teachers are able to clarify and understand the goals of the genre, joint construction creates opportunities for writers to engage with concepts such as invention, brainstorming, and expansion. The process also helps students develop stamina. Some students assume that for others, writing is an easy task. And for some of our students, this may be true. But ELL/multilingual writers are often surprised to learn that their monolingual peers have similar starts and stops as they write. The experience of composing as a class illustrates that most writers have the same concerns getting started and committing words to paper. It also illustrates the ways in which other class members approach a writing task. Do they start at the beginning? Do they start in the middle? How do they brainstorm? Joint deconstruction demonstrates that writing is a process, one that is not often as rigid or streamlined as some students believe it should be. Joint construction helps teachers and students realize this and even talk about it as the joint draft emerges.

Once students have settled on a topic, purpose, and audience for their text, the composing begins. Here Mrs. Keller led them to think about ideas and sentiments they might want to share with readers. She collected student ideas, often prodding them to turn those ideas into sentences. In the construction of the snow narrative, Mrs. Keller was eager to have students use sensory detail in their writing, so she used questions-and-cuing to ask students how they might describe the snow using their various senses—sight, sounds and voices, smells, the feel of a snowball, and so on. Students chimed in with ideas as Mrs. Keller and a student volunteer took notes on the board and also on a Google Doc. Students noted the costs of cars being towed, the sounds of their parents shoveling snow (voices, exclamations), and the number of days they were absent from school. As Mrs. Keller facilitated the discussion, she began to ask them how they might want to group ideas, and she asked them to consider their sentences. Slowly, a draft of three paragraphs, plus an introduction, began to emerge (see Figure 4.5). This was the first draft.

Every student in the class had added a detail, often bridging and building off of one another's comments and suggestions. After class, Mrs. Keller noted that even her most silent students had pointed out certain things about the piece. One student, for example, wanted to know where their teenage readers might read this; would the text be in a newspaper, in an op-ed section, or on a blog? Other students realized they might have to use metaphors or more figurative language to help readers outside New Hampshire understand the height and depth of the snow. One student complained that he didn't want the writing to be boring. The other students agreed and then decided that given their audience, they wanted to add some moments of humor to hold the readers' interest. The students were learning the craft of writing together.

Teaching Revision: Expansion

As the draft emerges from the students' combined efforts, so does a working artifact that can be used to teach revision and expansion. In Mrs. Keller's classroom on the following morning, a 24" × 36" poster of the students' draft, now titled "Snow in New Hampshire," hangs from the board. Students murmur; they have never seen their writing so large before. The teacher reminds them that it has to be big: the class has work to do on the draft today, and it's going to require them all to chip in. Class time is now dedicated to revision and expansion.

For many ELL/multilingual writers, the revision and expansion steps of the writing process are often shortchanged. These students have spent many years working on simply generating enough words and sentences to make a paragraph, and enough paragraphs to get the assignment done. More often than not, the writing instruction they have experienced in earlier grades concentrated primarily on the prewriting and drafting stages. Given the labor and time pressures that are often part of the process when writing in a second language, many ELL/multilingual writers have never learned how to set goals for revision or how to accomplish those goals. Joint construction offers the opportunity to see the ways their peers, their teachers, and other writers more generally refine, revise, and expand their drafts.

Figure 4.5. A joint construction draft of "Winter in New Hampshire," completed by students in a combined Google Doc.

Wow.
Dear Washington D.C.
We have had 5 tremendous snow days this February. We've also had three delays.We have so much snow there is no where to put it. Back in November, we have lost electricity during Thanksgiving.
Every snowstorm, we have had more than 2 feet.– For each snowstorm!! Four inches is nothing!

We've had to shovel all around our houses. It took more than an hour to do that. There is no ~~where~~place to put it. It is so bad that cars have had to be towed off the sidewalks and sides of streets. The parents of a few kids in our class had their cars towed. It cost them $150.00. They couldn't go to pick their car same day so they had to pay extra money too. It was horrible but we still went to school after two days.

Some people wear boots, scarf, hats and coat like big coat some kids wear two or three things jackets and coats and double socks. from what ~~I~~ observe out the window is the ground is white, you barely see any tree and its hard to see its impossible to describe snow.
Because there is a lot of snow and not a lot of space, we have big piles of snow that are around 18 ft high.–In some houses when you look out the window all you see is snow and snow trucks. At night when you try to sleep, is almost impossible because all you can hear is snow trucks, it's like if you were at Las Vegas: never quite! When you try to leave your driveway it's like fighting to get out of bed, almost impossible. There is too much snow in the driveway that you have to get up early just to shovel!

Other details from our brainstorming:
- Landlord had to send special people to shovel the snow~~?~~, b-eca~~(why?)~~use
- ~~T~~the snow from all the storms is now three times Gabriel's heigh~~t (how tall is Gabriel?)~~(approx:16 feet). Gabriel's like 5ft 5 inches.
- The highest snow pile is at the Elementary school.
- Mom's and dad's are arguing about the snow and their cars being towed.– "It was a disaster."
- you wouldn't be able to drive because its not safe.
- The mood of people in New Hampshire is cranky. Skiers like it. Other people are irritated, mad, tired.
- Sounds= loud sounds= plow trucks/icicles breaking and crashing on cars.
- What does it look like out the windows? so bright and white.
- Feel (on skin, on hands, on eyes): 11 degrees Fahrenheit/No one can move/Feel frozen. What do we have to wear? We have to wear a jacket, gloves,boots

Mrs. Keller writes the word *REVISION* on the board. She encourages students to break down the word—*RE* and *VISION*—noting that the prefix *RE* means "to do again." She explains that revision means to "re-see" a piece of writing. During revision, writers add, reuse, recycle, move, unbury ideas and stories, add details, expand, and fill in the gaps. In addition to the poster-size draft, she hands out regular-size copies of the "Snow in New Hampshire" draft so that each student has a tangible copy to engage with at their desks. She wants to have the large-print version at the front of the classroom so that students can come up to work on the revision, but she also doesn't want students to disengage because they can't see the draft from the back of the room. Mrs. Keller wants them to be able to write down ideas or make changes on the draft, even if they aren't sure they want to share those with the class right away.

Once all students have copies and are settled, Mrs. Keller asks them to quick-write for two minutes: "Okay, let's do some writing. Read it over. What is one thing that you really like about this piece?"

A student responds, "We never tell the reader who we are. We use *we* all over, but they don't know who we are. I think that is a problem. Why would they keep reading?"

Mrs. Keller replies, "Excellent—you are thinking like a writer. Great point."

Another student chimes in, "I think we need some better sentences."

As students settle into the work of locating and creating better sentences, Ali, who's from Iraq, goes up to the board and writes the following: "People are so tired of snow, so tired of shoveling, so tired of the accidents caused by snow." As he reads it aloud to the class, there are "whoa's" and a long whistle. Students offer praise: "Man, I didn't know you could write like that." "We got to include that." (See Figure 4.6.)

Mrs. Keller builds on this praise and then explains why the sentence works so well: "It's great, isn't it? Ali, your use of repetition: so tired, so tired, so tired. It's lyrical, like poetry. Simply beautiful." Ali beams, and the class begins to discuss where his sentence should go in the draft, asking one another where it will have the most impact on readers.

Two other students, Shaina and Liz, head to the Big Paper version of the class draft and begin to ask other students to repeat their other ideas for descriptions and sentences. Soon the whole class is directing Shaina and Liz about where to add new sentences and details and suggesting new word choices and endings for the draft. Over the course of the class period, a more developed essay begins to emerge (see Figure 4.7).

Figure 4.6. Using a Big Paper version of the joint construction and student input to teach and demonstrate the messiness of revision and critical thinking that is part of improving our writing.

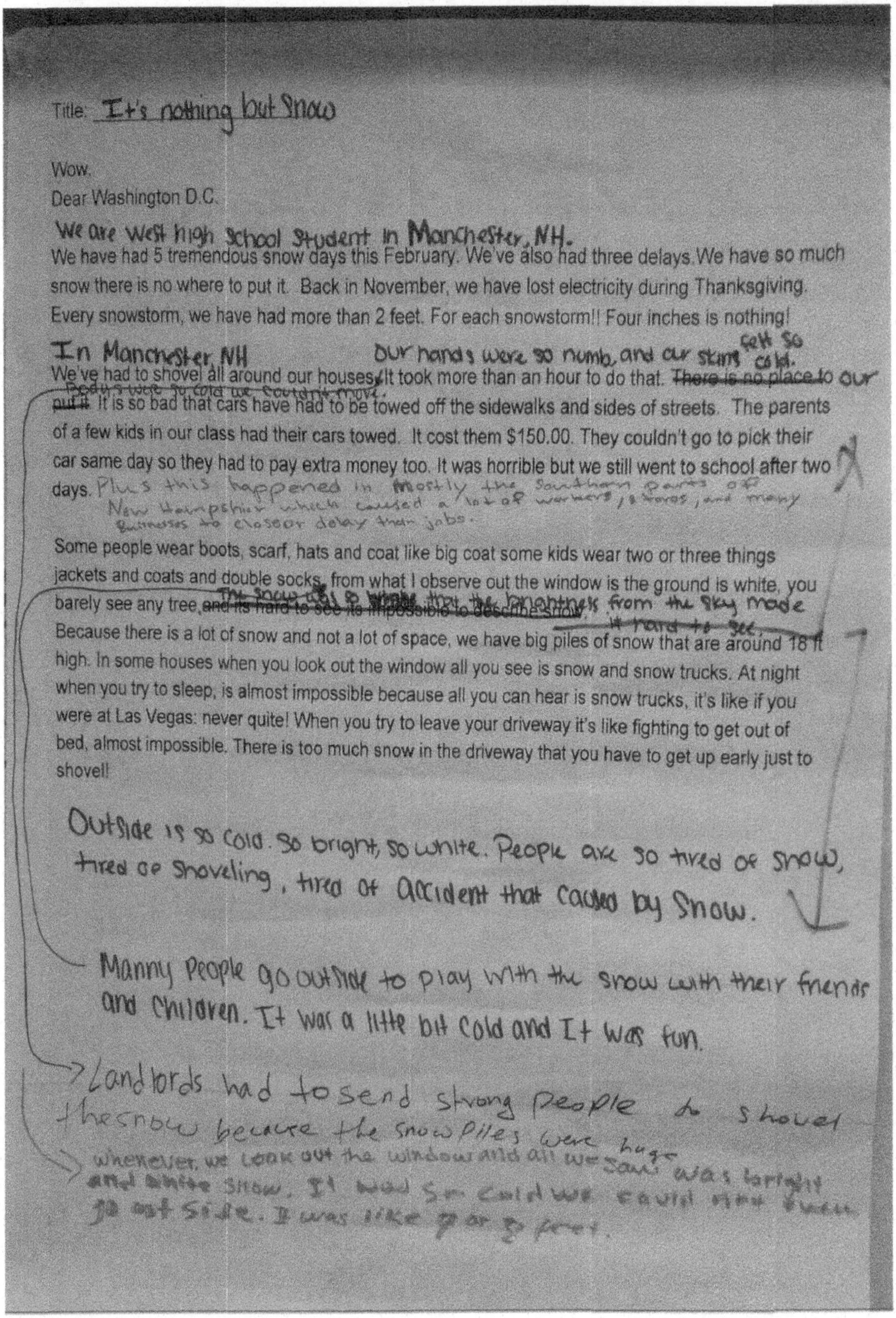

Figure 4.7. A more expansive and complete essay emerges.

It's Nothing But Snow!

Wow.
Dear Washington D.C.,

We are West High School students in Manchester, New Hampshire. We have had 5 tremendous snow days this February. We've also had three delays. We have so much snow there is no where to put it. Back in November, we have lost electricity during Thanksgiving. Every snowstorm, we have had more than 2 feet. For each snowstorm!! Four inches is nothing!

In Manchester, New Hampshire, we've had to shovel all around our houses. It took more than an hour to do that. It is so bad that cars have had to be towed off the sidewalks and sides of streets. Landlords have had to send strong people to shovel snow because the snow piles were huge. The parents of a few kids in our class had their cars towed. It cost them $150.00. They couldn't go to pick their car same day so they had to pay extra money too. It was horrible but we still went to school after two days. Plus, this all happened in mostly the southern part of New Hampshire which caused a lot of workers, stores, and many businesses to close or delay their jobs.

Because there is a lot of snow and not a lot of space, we have big piles of snow that are around 18 ft high. In some houses when you look out the window all you see is snow and snow trucks. At night when you try to sleep, is almost impossible because all you can hear is snow trucks, it's like if you were at Las Vegas: never quiet! When you try to leave your driveway it's like fighting to get out of bed, almost impossible. There is too much snow in the driveway that you have to get up early just to shovel!

Our hands were numb, and our skins felt so cold. Our bodies were so cold we couldn't move. Outside is so cold. So bright and white. People feel sad, tired, and unhappy. People are so tired of snow, so tired of shoveling, so tired of the accidents caused by snow. Some students didn't like snow because it's very hard to walk outside in the morning time.

Some people wear boots, scarf, hats and coat like big coat some kids wear two or three layers of jackets and coats and double socks. From what we observe out the window is that the ground is white, you barely see any trees. The snow was so white that the brightness from the sky made it hard to see.

Many people went outside to play in the snow with their friends and children. It was a bit cold, but it was fun. And few people stayed inside because of outside coldness. Little kids were engaging on snow fights.

In conclusion, this is the worst winter ever.

Teaching Revision: Language Usage and Grammar

Joint construction can also provide teachers with moments to talk about language usage, including figurative language, grammar, and specific sentence structures. Teaching grammar is an important part of any ELA classroom, and for student writers, style and language usage are important considerations as they learn their craft as writers. Unfortunately, for many ELL/multilingual writers, the bulk of their grammar and language instruction is often caught up in worksheets and rote memorization. There is a long-standing belief that students need to master these "basics" before they can write meaningful prose. The difficulty is that they are rarely given the opportunity to move beyond the worksheets and single-sentence answers. Another problem is that even mastery of these structures and rules in worksheets and quizzes doesn't often translate into their written texts. For many ELL/multilingual students, the worksheets are one task and their writing is another, with a real sense of disconnection between the two.

An SFL approach to writing helps teachers begin to bridge the gap between students' meaningful writing practices and discussions about grammar and style. The recursivity of the approach encourages teachers and students to return to the model texts they used in deconstruction, as well as the model text they themselves created through their joint construction, to refine sentence and language choices. The oral discussions that have preceded these lessons create a classroom context that allows everyone to talk about grammar and language choices in ways that relate to earlier conversations about a writer's choices, purpose, and perhaps more important, audience. Teachers can also use these discussions about language to share not only the rules but also the options. Rarely is there only one way to craft a sentence or to express a sentiment, and students need experiences in vetting their options and thinking through which language choices and sentence constructions will work best under specific circumstances. For example, is a long, winding lyrical sentence more appropriate, or is it better to be short, succinct, and clear? As one student noted, the "correct" language choice for an audience of grown-ups may not be the "best" language choice for an audience of teenage hip-hop fans.

Mrs. Keller begins the second day of revision with the new draft on the projector for the whole class to see. She also asks students to pull out their sample model texts. Today's goal is to have the class pay more attention to specific language and style issues. For example, she explores the active voice in sentences and draws attention to transitions and punctuation for dialogue. These are points of concern—language traits and grammatical features—that Mrs. Keller has identified from what she has seen in the students' other written work, the standards employed by her district for this grade level, and the language goals she has set for this narrative unit. She uses sections from the model essays consulted during deconstruction (which are now familiar and require no new vocabulary lessons) and the students' own joint construction to demonstrate language rules and conventions. She then has pairs of students take a paragraph from the class essay to revise, and they edit paragraph by paragraph, before returning to the whole class to share their suggestions and ideas.

At another point, Mrs. Keller decides to teach students how to write and punctuate dialogue. The discussion begins with an overview of how dialogue can add to character development, create a sense of action and reaction, and move narratives forward. Students again look at excerpts from the model text used in their joint reconstruction. Mrs. Keller then has each of them write sample dialogue that is connected to their "Snow in New Hampshire" essay, drawing their attention to the punctuation. In the argument unit that follows, she will remind students of this lesson as she teaches them how to use and punctuate quotations from primary and secondary sources.

The Merits of Joint Construction

Because of the time crunch all teachers face, teachers may be tempted to either move quickly through joint construction into independent construction (the next stage in the SFL approach) or to skip joint construction altogether. However, skipping this step often leaves ELL/multilingual students less prepared to write independently. They haven't had much opportunity to try out phrasing or strategies, nor have weaker writers gained knowledge and skills from watching more experienced writers take risks or offering input on a class-constructed version of the genre. In the end, skipping the joint construction stage may result in students producing weaker texts and teachers spending more time helping them generate material. In response to these very real time concerns, I suggest that teachers consider teaching fewer writing units but add more depth and time to those units. In addition, as students become more familiar with the SFL approach and the elements of deconstruction and joint construction, the questions they need to be asking about a writing task or genre and the decisions they need to make as writers come more quickly.

Stage 3. Independent Construction: Becoming Writers

Building on the confidence, strategies, and discussions that emerge from the joint construction, the next goal is independent construction. Students take what they have learned, discussed, and modeled as a class of writers and each composes his or her own narrative or essay. In line with most teaching writing methods, Mrs. Keller uses brainstorming, listing, and quickwrites to help her students develop topics and ideas for their own constructions. She may even draw on what she knows about her students from their literacy maps to help them choose and develop topics they feel connected to. A few will decide to choose a topic that is closely related to the one completed by the class during joint construction. Others will have been inspired by the conversations thus far or ideas they have written about in their journals. Many of them will be eager to move on to their own writing, confident from having watched the process unfold in class and confident about the expectations of the genre, the readers, and the possibilities.

For most students, the joint construction will have given them some ideas about how to start, as well as examples of the kinds of traits and conventions they want to include in their own stories and essays. More reluctant and hesitant writers have observed the decisions and composing processes of more experienced, confident peers. Perhaps they have had opportunities to contribute some of their own insights to the conversations along the way. The expectations and the process of getting words to paper have become more transparent.

During independent construction, teachers encourage students to use strategies for revision similar to those they employed as a class during the joint construction phase. Mrs. Keller might, for example, ask students to highlight their noun choices and consider stronger use of details or imagery. In the narrative unit, she might ask them to think about places where they can help readers "feel like they were there" and help them work on writing scenes with more sensory detail or dialogue. She might even encourage them to share large paper drafts with small groups of peers and listen to suggestions for expansion, for adding clarity, or for being more poetic. As part of the independent construction stage, teachers also provide opportunities for response and feedback from readers; the next chapter explores specific recommendations for responding to ELL/multilingual writers' texts and building effective peer response opportunities into the writing classroom.

The independent construction phase also allows teachers to intervene through mini-lessons and mini-writing activities, when needed. Here are two examples of those kinds of intervention:

> • **Mini-lessons and returning to model texts.** Teachers may find it helpful to return to model texts and deconstruction activities to address specific concerns or highlight certain text traits. These mini-lessons can be a good way to return to finer points of writing that students may have overlooked earlier on, such as transitions between paragraphs or even punctuation. For example, Mrs. Keller noticed students struggling with verb tense shifts as they were drafting their independent pieces. One morning, as part of a ten-minute mini lesson, she placed a copy of the

model text on the board and asked students about the author's use of verb tenses for a flashback. During the argument unit, she held a mini-lesson to demonstrate how writers punctuate and cite quotations and other types of evidence that students included in their essays.

• **Mimics and templated phrasing.** Mimicry is another option to help ELL students try on language and phrasing that may seem outside of their experience. One of the most valuable and memorable writing assignments I was given as a younger writer was to choose a scene or moment from the novel we were reading and write "the forgotten scene," an assignment that asked me to emulate and mimic the moves of a professional writer. The assignment created a visceral experience for me as a writer, one that would stay with me when I approached my own writing projects. A part of this activity felt wildly transgressive to me as a young writer—imaginative, and also scary. But looking back, the exercise required me to conduct a fair amount of genre analysis. To write like Thomas Mann, I had to study and be attentive to how Mann constructed sentences and paragraphs, built characters, and started paragraphs: his long meandering sentences, his entrances into dialogue, his descriptions, and so on. Through this activity, I learned how to use a published author as a kind of mentor. The activity had me "lean on" Mann's style in order to try something new, and in the process, I discovered new possibilities and new depth for my own written work and ideas.

In the college textbook *They Say/I Say: The Moves That Matter in Academic Writing*, Gerald Graff and Cathy Birkenstein (2010) make the point that mimicking needn't always be seen as a bad thing. They offer templated sentence patterns for argument, comparison, and disagreements. In my own research, I've often have found that ELL/multilingual writers struggle with the openings to new sentences and paragraphs. The connective tissue of transitional phrases and the ways in which authors introduce new ideas or material seem unnatural; after all, we rarely have a need for these kinds of segues in oral conversation. For most writers, these are learned skills gained from extensive reading and experience. But while inexperienced writers may understand the need for transitions and connections, they may also feel that they don't own the language or have the depth of experience as writers and readers to employ such devices in their own writing. Samples and templates of certain kinds of sentences can help them get started. As with any scaffolding device, teachers need to be conscious of how often they use this type of support with their students.

A Note of Caution

Templates, like the continual use of graphic organizers for ELL students, can sometimes hinder students as much as help them. For some students, templates become a support that they cling to and feel paralyzed without. As a result, they never have an opportunity to develop their confidence or to trust their critical thinking skills as writers. Our goal in using scaffolding tools should be to keep moving toward fewer tools and more student confidence with writing. That sense of confidence comes from successfully navigating a piece of writing and working through the various aspects—both frustrating and rewarding—in order to feel triumphant, empowered with strategies, and a sense of completion. In short, ELL/multilingual writers need opportunities to craft their written texts. These experiences, when paired with proper support and responsive instructional approaches, encourage them to see themselves as real writers with ownership and investment in their words, opinions, arguments, and stories.

In the next chapter, I take up the issue of support more fully by considering teacher response and the importance of feedback. I look closely at how teachers can build feedback cycles into the teaching-learning cycles of joint and independent writing construction, and how teachers can adapt their response practices to provide more effective assistance to the ELL and multilingual writers in their classrooms.

Responding to ELL Writers and Their Texts

Miguel

Miguel hands in a final draft of his essay to his ELA teacher in mid-November. He is one of six ELL and former ELL students in this sophomore English class. Miguel came to the United States from the Dominican Republic about two years ago, when he was in seventh grade. His conversational English is quite good, but he still struggles with reading and writing. In his notebooks, one can see him working on his reading and writing, meticulously copying out numerous passages from the books he reads for class in an attempt to translate and understand the readings. He admits that writing and reading in English are difficult; these days, though, even writing and reading in Spanish are difficult. Outside of class, Miguel likes copying out his ELA teachers' notes and words from books he reads for class because he has confidence that the words he is copying are "right"; they aren't his own and they are written by native English speakers. There is something comforting about copying down passages that helps him feel more competent about writing, and his notebooks are filled with long paragraphs from science books, short stories, and even novels. Three days a week,

Miguel takes part in an ELL class down the hall that provides him with homework help. The paper he is handing in to his teacher is the lengthiest assignment he and his peers have had to complete since school started in September.

When he receives the paper back, Miguel is confused. There is a tallied score at the top of the page and four words circled in red. In one section, an entire sentence has been crossed out, and the letters *AWK* are written in the margin. No other comments, no suggestions for future essays, no input on sentence structure, and no remarks on the content. When Miguel meets with me, he isn't quite sure what to make of these marks. He reports, "I think it is good. That essay." He tells me he is happy with his grade, a high *C*. As I ask what he might want to work on next time, he points to the four circled words and the crossed out sentence. "These." He explains that he guesses that these are the only things he needs to do next time around. When I ask Miguel about the teacher's marks on his paper, he isn't sure why those words are circled or why the sentence has been crossed out. But he confides to me that his strategy for writing next time will include not using those circled words again.

The Importance of Feedback

For ELL and multilingual writers like Miguel to succeed in writing, effective teacher feedback and response is essential. Teacher written feedback "plays a central role" in the development of ELL/multilingual writers (Hyland, 2003, p. 178). It is an important instructional tool that allows teachers to give students a degree of individual attention to their ongoing development as writers and English learners. Yet the kinds of feedback that are often given to ELL/multilingual writers can be problematic, and many teachers are unsure about the best practices in this aspect of writing instruction. In this chapter, I take up the concerns of ELA teachers when they are reviewing an ELL writer's' text. My method here is to separate the threads of teacher response that we typically link together—response to content, response to error, and grading/evaluation—so that we can consider how the strategies around each of these kinds of teacher feedback can become instructional moments for students, as well as for teachers. I also consider how teachers can build feedback cycles into writing instruction and structure more participatory and empowering peer review sessions for diverse classes.

Teacher Perspectives on Response

The *NCTE Position Paper on the Role of English Teachers in Educating English Language Learners* suggests the following practices for teacher response:

- Offer comments on the strength of the paper to indicate areas where the student is meeting expectations.
- Make comments explicit and clear (in both written and oral responses). Teachers should consider beginning feedback with global comments (content and ideas, organization, thesis) and then move on to more local concerns (or mechanical errors) when student writers are more confident with the content of their drafts.
- Give more than one suggestion for change so that students maintain control of their writing.

For many teachers, these suggestions already parallel their practices with student writers, whether they are monolingual English speakers or multilinguals. I want to expand on these principles to consider how ELA teachers can begin to implement these suggestions in ways that provide more instructional opportunities and support for the ELL/multilingual writers in their classrooms.

Most of the questions I hear when I work with content area teachers about multilingual writers are related to response, correction, and grading:

- "How do I correct an ELL writer's paper?"
- "Do I correct everything?"
- "How do I prioritize?"
- "I know they have important ideas to share, but there are so many other concerns that I have and that they have to deal with here."
- "What about grammar and mechanics?"
- "I don't see any change in their writing; do they even pay attention to my marks or feedback?"
- "What is fair?"

Throughout this book, my goal is to help teachers think through assignments and instructional approaches that benefit all students: a universal design approach. But responding to the written work of multilingual students is one area of writing instruction that requires teachers to consider more deliberate "ELL-friendly" strategies.

In the education courses and workshops I teach, I find that teachers are always at a bit of a loss when I share copies of ELL/multilingual student work. When teachers look at these sample student papers, they generally focus on the language issues and writing concerns that multilingual writers are still trying to master—rather than on the ideas the students are trying to convey. Areas of written accent and even errors in language use that can be negotiated in conversations and oral communication seem far more blatant to English teachers when they see them on the written page. And it isn't just about grammar and mechanics; teachers focus on places in a student's text where genre expectations, organizational patterns, or tone are disrupted. As I discussed in Chapters 1 and 2, it's important to realize that many times American English teachers' expectations are shaped by cultural expectations and even rhetorical expectations that are different from those of their multilingual students. The shaping of a cohesive and well-executed argument in one country or culture is not necessarily the same in another (Connor, 1996; Li, 2005). So what seems different may not actually be wrong. Indeed, many of our expectations of language and writing are shaped by our cultural experiences, educational backgrounds and customs, and the training we've had as both teachers and former students. Concepts of "good writing" and genre, even in business and the professional worlds, are culturally constructed. What we often see as fixed concepts of good professional and workplace writing still vary from one country to the next, even if the professionals in those countries are all using English in their correspondence. The problem is that we generally teach our expectations of genre, conventions, organization, and tone as fixed and universal to the students in our ELA classrooms.

ELA teachers often have one of two reactions when reading an ELL writer's text: either (1) they overcorrect or (2) they feel unsure about where to even begin and thus avoid correction altogether (Ferris & Hedgcock, 2014; Ortmeier-Hooper, 2013). When overcorrection occurs, ELA teachers tend to feel the "pull of the pen" and the need to "straighten" out a student's language, syntax, and spelling by replacing words and even reconstructing full sentences. Many teachers read multilinguals' texts with a sense of awkwardness, wanting to eliminate certain

The "Pull of the Pen"

I often recommend that ELA and ELL teachers make copies of ELL/multilingual students' papers if they feel the "pull of the pen" when they respond. For some teachers, putting down the pen and just reading student work feels almost impossible to do. They sometimes comment that it slows down or even hinders their reading (of any text) when they can't annotate as they read. With the two-copies approach, teachers can annotate as they need to on the copy, and then they can make more calculated, thoughtful decisions about the comments they want to include on the draft that is returned to the student.

The only caveat to this advice is that I encourage teachers to use their pens to note the positive moments alongside the critiques and corrections. Read with an eye toward praiseworthy constructions, innovative metaphors or imagery, elegant titles or introductions, effective use of evidence or personal story, and so on. Look for what the writer does well, including use of particular vocabulary, punctuation, sentence structures, transitions, and more. Be open to what works well or captures your attention as a reader, even if it doesn't follow the norms set by monolingual writers.

constructions, rewrite word choices, and correct punctuation, verb tense, preposi-
tions, etc. My own sense is that this "pull of the pen" is generally well intentioned,
and in some cases, it's done somewhat unconsciously. English teachers, practiced
in the art of reading complicated texts, annotate their way through student papers,
trying to make sense and construct meaning by reshaping or marking the words on
the page. The problem with this approach, intentional or unintentional, is that it
leaves student writers with an annotated copy of their writing that can be difficult
to decipher and overwhelming for some ELLs. Such annotation often overlooks
the meaning (or imagery or argument or poetic language) the student is trying to
construct. But the second reaction to the written work of ELLs—not responding
or providing feedback at all—is also not the answer. Avoiding response is not helpful, and it's unfair to the many ELL/multilingual writers who are interested in how
to improve and in what others (particularly teacher readers) think of their ideas and
their work.

How Do ELL/Multilingual Writers View Teacher Feedback?

The spectrum of student response to teacher feedback is vast. Some reactions are
shaped by years of frustration, while others arise from a kind of hopelessness that
surrounds students' experiences with second language writing. On the positive end
of the spectrum, some students relish the teacher's input and are eager to make
changes. Overwhelmingly, though, research tells us that ELL/multilingual students
value teacher feedback (Ferris, 2002; Kibler, 2011).

   In many studies, high school ELL students report that they receive very
little feedback from teachers on the strength of their prose or ideas, and they are
often unsure how to interpret the few markings that teachers leave on their papers
(Villalva, 2006a, 2006b; Ferris, 2006). These student concerns are compounded
by the fact that many English language and multilingual learners feel anonymous
in their content area classrooms; they feel their teachers don't know them and
therefore engage with their written work through the lens of errors. High school
ELL students like Miguel often share frustrating, disheartening experiences with
written teacher comments, or lack thereof. Miguel, for one, was never sure whether
his teacher even read his work—she either corrected it or attached a rubric with
categories circled to indicate which areas he needed to attend to. For Miguel, this
wasn't enough support, instructionally or emotionally. He struggled to get good
grades, often taking tests and writing assignments to his ELL teacher, who corrected the pages and then sent him off to rewrite or edit them. As the year went on,
he became more and more reluctant to complete or share his writing assignments.

   Teacher response is important, not only because it provides a tangible way
to offer students much needed individual attention, but also because it can create a

conversational exchange that helps teachers develop rapport and relationships with students who may feel marginalized in the classroom. Teachers' comments can also be motivational, helping students generate a stronger interest in writing. In a study of teacher response and motivation, Lipstein and Renninger note that it was important for students to "continue to feel positively about writing" (p. 136). They explain that "once [students'] confidence in their own knowledge and abilities increased, their interest in writing deepened. . . . By contrast, students who received feedback that was too discrepant (e.g., too abstract, or requiring a lot of work) often spoke of becoming less engaged in writing as a result" (p. 136). If the act of writing makes ELL students feel silenced and hesitant, a teacher's response can either shut that student writer down further or propel that student to become more invested in his or her own words. But as second language specialist Ken Hyland (2003) explains, "teachers need to consider what students want from feedback and what they attend to in their revisions" (p. 179).

Providing Effective Feedback: When, Where, and How

In Chapter 4, I discussed the importance of the instructional cycle in writing instruction. Here, I offer a similar way of thinking about feedback and feedback delivery. In particular, I divide the feedback cycle into two distinct discussions: one on teacher written and oral response and one on error correction. This is a purposeful decision. In many ways, the distinction I am drawing here counters concerns that content area teachers too often respond only to the texts of ELL and multilingual writers by marking errors, rather than commenting on their ideas or offering suggestions to deepen or develop their writing.

Building a Feedback Cycle

For teachers, seeing feedback as part of a cycle can be a helpful way to think through comments, corrections, and timing (Ferris & Hedgcock, 2013). The goal of a feedback cycle is to help teachers offer response at well-chosen moments in the composing process and find opportunities when students can move toward becoming better readers of their own work. For the most part, experts recommend that teachers take a two-step approach to responding to the written texts of ELL/ multilingual students, with the first round of feedback focused on encouraging idea development, organization, refining descriptions or points of evidence, and expansion. Teachers should then create a second round of feedback that concentrates on mechanics, grammar, and other language-based concerns. This parallels discussions about offering global feedback focused on "higher-order concerns" (HOCs)

A Sample Feedback Cycle

During Joint Construction

- Feedback to the whole class on their collaboratively written text. Teacher incorporates opportunities for the class to decide how to respond and address the teacher's points.

- Whole-class mini-lessons (teachers might return to deconstructing certain passages from model texts or the class joint construction to provide examples).

During Individual Construction
First Draft

- Teacher written comments, focused on helping students clarify and build on the strengths of their texts.

- Peer feedback (see page 109 for advice on building better peer feedback sessions).

- Whole-class mini-lessons (teachers might return to deconstructing certain passages from model texts or the class joint construction to provide examples).

Second Draft (written comments or teacher-student conference)

- Selective feedback on improving accuracy in language, grammar, and mechanics (see pages 105–8 for more advice on this kind of feedback).

Final Draft

- Student's self-reflection on written text and student's ideas about what he or she wants to work on in the next writing assignment.

- Teacher feedback, focused on what has worked well for the student in this assignment and also with suggestions for developing even further as a writer in the next assignment.

first and then offering local feedback focused on "lower-order concerns" (LOCs) second, a framework that is often used to help new teachers learn how to respond to student writing in general. While I value this approach, I also realize that differentiating between HOCs and LOCs can feel more difficult to unravel when working with ELL/multilingual writers. As Dana Ferris (2003) has noted, there are moments when lower-order concerns make a passage of student text difficult to understand and interrupt meaning in ways that leave the teacher confused about the student's ideas. One guiding principle for teachers, then, is to prioritize feedback and to consider which concerns interrupt understanding and meaning.

Reading with an Open Mind

Paul Kei Matsuda and Michelle Cox (2011) remind teachers that keeping an open mind while reading the texts of multilingual writers is essential:

> Some of the initial reactions to ESL writers' texts may be quite positive. Inexperienced readers of ESL texts may be fascinated by details about the ESL writer's native language, culture, or country, or stories of how they or their family came to the United States. Some may be intrigued by the extensive use of metaphors and figurative language in some ESL writers' texts. Others may be amazed by how much the writers have accomplished with a language they did not grow up with. Unfortunately, not all encounters with ESL texts produce such generous responses. Readers with little or no experience in working with ESL writers may be drawn to surface-level errors and differences that they see as problematic. (pp. 4–5).

Teachers may find differences between the texts of monolingual English students and those of multilingual students in their classes, from word choices or the use of certain idioms to errors in sentence structures or verb endings. In addition, some students may be reluctant to express an opinion, even if the assignment asks them to do so, or they may have different approaches to organization or thesis statement placement that are not formulaic but are perhaps more innovative and still effective. The key for teachers is to remain generous and open as they work through a student's draft. Sometimes particular aspects of a student's intention or reader questions will become clearer or resolved as the teacher keeps reading.

It is helpful to remember that, as the original Conference on College Composition and Communication (CCCC) *Statement on Teaching Second Language Writing and Writers* stated, "[T]he acquisition of a second language and second language literacy is a time-consuming process that will continue through students' academic careers and beyond" (2001). As teachers, we cannot bring ELL writers "up to speed" with one round of corrections and comments. Even if students attend to every mark the teacher makes, that doesn't necessarily mean they are learning to be better writers or that they are developing the confidence and self-sufficiency that will guide them in their future writing activities. It's important to see feedback as ongoing and as one part of a larger process and writing instruction philosophy. Many second language writers will continue to "acquire syntactic and lexical competence" throughout their lives (CCCC, 2009). Similarly, some students may not be able to hear or even see errors or concerns on their own; the old adage "'read it aloud to hear your errors'" may not be very useful to ELL/multilingual writers. Even if students have done well on grammar tests and rules, they may not have internalized those rules to apply to their own writing. Developing these skills takes time, and teachers may find that they need to offer students tangible strategies to help them develop those skills.

Writing with an Accent

In our communities, we are often tolerant of nonnative speakers who continue to speak with an accent. My mother, an immigrant from Germany, speaks English fluently, but even fifty years after coming to the United States, she continues to have an accent. In her oral communications with others, most people are fairly forgiving of her speech, even when she misses articles, misuses a preposition, or makes a mistake in her pronunciation. When she tells stories of her childhood or shares the latest gossip about family in Germany, her accent thickens and becomes infused with colorful phrases and German idioms. In these moments, her accent does not distract; it actually pulls those around her closer because they are eager to hear and experience the stories she shares.

We often see this kind of accented English in written work too. For example, we relish and praise the literary works of Isabel Allende, Gloria Anzaldúa, and others who use their mother tongues and their own innovations with English to deepen the experiences of readers and pull us more closely into their worlds.

But in classrooms, many teachers are reluctant to embrace the written accents of their ELL and multilingual students. Often, the "pull of the pen," coupled with a sense of duty (we are English teachers, after all), compels us to erase and correct all evidence of a student's accent on the page. In some instances, our dedication can work against us and our students. When teachers try to erase students' accents, students may feel these efforts as attempts to erase their voices. By not thinking about the role of written accent in a student's text, teachers can discourage ELL/multilingual writers' attempts to share certain experiences, to create deliberate cross-cultural moments and reactions from readers, and to draw readers more closely into their worlds. In short, there may be moments when a multilingual writer's accent on the page actually matches the genre, the audience, and the intent of the writer. Furthermore, some marks of "accented English" may not actually be grammatically incorrect; they may just seem odd or new.

Approaching feedback with the knowledge of written accent in mind can help teachers remain more open-minded and help them think through the questions they may want to ask young writers about their texts, as well as the suggestions for revision that would be most beneficial.

Specific Response Strategies for ELL/Multilingual Writers

> There is an art to providing effective feedback.
> —Ferris & Hedgcock (2013, p. 252)

The best way for teachers to respond to ELL/multilingual writers is to keep in mind these general approaches: be selective, thoughtful, clear, and personal. Beyond these qualities of response, though, are some more specific strategies for teachers to employ.

1. *Read the entire draft or paper before making comments.*
Matsuda and Cox (2011) suggest that readers focus on "what the writer is trying to communicate and how the paper is organized" (p. 11) as they read, and that they read all the way to the end before making marks or commenting. If you don't read all the way to the end, you may make a comment and then find that the student addresses that concern later in the paper. You could also miss out on information that helps illuminate the student's meaning and makes the student's organization patterns more discernable. But as Matsuda and Cox note, "[R]eading to the end of a piece of ESL writing is only beneficial if the reader can suspend judgment while reading—reading past variations in sentence structure, waiting to see how the writer will pull the paper together, maintaining an open mind when the writer's opinions and beliefs vary substantially" from reader's (p. 11).

On a practical note, when you comment on your first read of a student paper, it's difficult to be selective and prioritize the feedback. By reading the entire paper first, you have an opportunity to think through which concerns are most pressing.

2. *Be selective and prioritize.*
You should not address every concern at once. It can be helpful to chart growth and your goals for the ELL/multilinguals in your class in a notebook or journal, but know that students can become overwhelmed with too many comments and corrections. At a certain point, that feeling of being overwhelmed becomes counterproductive. Even if students "fix" all the places you mark, they may be doing so in a "teacher fixes, I change" manner that doesn't lead to learning or investment in the writing.

Most L2 writing specialists suggest sticking with two to three concerns that you would like students to work on for an individual revision or draft. If you have comments for the final draft, try to offer suggestions about what the student can carry into the next assignment. Such suggestions help students think about how different writing assignments and genres are connected, and understand that writers transfer what they have learned from one experience to the next writing experience. These comments on final drafts should include encouraging suggestions for students to repeat specific things they have done well and also concrete suggestions for how they might build on those skills in the next assignment.

3. *Ask questions and see comments as part of a conversation with the student writer.*
If you are confused about a particular passage, use of a word, or the wording of a sentence, ask the student orally. Sometimes teachers correct a sentence prematurely without understanding the student's intention or meaning. In these cases, it can be far more effective to ask the student a question, either in a short conference or in the margin of the paper.

Many ELL and multilingual students are quite good at clarifying their points orally, and often that conversation with the teacher can help them generate language to clarify those points on the page. Try to inquire about the student's' intent and explain what aspect of the text is confusing to you as a reader. Emphasize that you are confused as a reader in order to heighten the student writer's understanding of audience and intent, not just correction.

Ask questions that connect back to readers and the writer's purpose. Help students realize that writing is not just a matter of correct grammar or well-chosen vocabulary. Often you can encourage ELLs/ multilinguals to refine or expand on their essays by asking questions about how they understand their readers/intended audience, or how what they wrote matches their purpose. Again, many of these questions may mirror the in-class dialogues that are part of the deconstruction and joint construction cycles mentioned in Chapter 4.

Also ask questions about interesting moments. On one occasion, I was working with a high school student from Taiwan who purposefully used quotations from a family member in his essay. He was particularly proud of the use of actual dialogue and his attempts at punctuating dialogue. He was trying to help readers "hear" the voice of this family member to make their experiences of reading his essay more memorable. When his teacher crossed out the quotations because of punctuation errors, the student couldn't understand why. He also felt that she hadn't even noticed his attempts at innovation and detail. This student's experience and concerns are not uncommon, and as teachers we have all had moments when we overlooked a student's risk-taking and saw only the mistake. My rule of thumb these days is to be on the lookout for these attempts at innovation and to try to see them through the lens of "half full" rather than "half empty."

   4. *Look for moments to praise.*
As you read, look for moments to praise. What is the writer doing well? It may be the use of a specific new vocabulary word. It may a beautiful description or image. It might be an excellent point in an argument, or the use of a personal example that drives home a point in ways you hadn't considered. It might be the successful integration of a quote or a particularly poignant question in the introduction or conclusion. Look for these moments. Praise them. If possible, try to explain to students why these moments are successful. It may be that you are just excited to see a student successfully trying out a new sentence structure or word. It might be that the student successfully implemented an idea mentioned in class. It might be the correct use of a semicolon or a well-punctuated sentence.

Try to be specific about the praise. "Good" and "Very interesting" are vague comments, and if the goal is to encourage students to build on their strengths, then we need to try to explain what the strength is and why it works well for readers or the writer's purpose.

5. *Be clear.*

In the opening to this chapter, Miguel expressed his confusion at the teacher's marks and codes like *AWK* on his paper. He is not alone. Even when teachers supply their students with a key for certain marks or corrections, many ELL writers are new to these codes. Even if some have encountered these kinds of coding systems before, they are often unsure what they mean or how the concerns should be addressed. And more often than not, they are afraid to ask. So even if the teacher had written out *Awkward* in the margins of Miguel's paper, he might not have known what the actual problem was with his sentence. Was it the verb tense, the sentence structure, the misuse of a prepositional phrase, or something else? What is it exactly that makes a sentence or phrase "awkward" 'to readers? What suggestions might his teacher give Miguel to help him address "awkwardness," especially given that he is writing in his second or third language? The same concerns are also inherent in phrases like "Be more clear" or "Unclear." Quite simply, teachers need to supply a greater sense of context and be more precise in their written comments. Try to keep comments and individual sentences clear and easy to follow. Provide examples (e.g., from model texts) when possible.

6. *Make comments readable.*

Think about the language you use to deliver comments. Are the students familiar with terms such as *subject-verb agreement, thesis statement,* and *conclusion?* If students don't understand the terms you use, you need to provide explanations and also examples that students can imitate.

Comments should also be easy to read. Some ELL/multilingual students struggle to read the teacher's handwriting, both on the board and in the comments on an assignment. Consider dividing comments and suggestions into bulleted points or a numbered list. Sometimes a teacher's lengthy prose or letter can be difficult to follow, and, more important, students may miss the finer points of the teacher's suggestions for improvement as they pour over the letter. When I do write longer response letters to students, I tend to combine these approaches by opening my letter with some prose and then using bullet points to draw their attention to specific points of praise and requests for revision.

7. *Offer more than one suggestion.*

Helping ELLs/multilinguals to invest in and engage with their writing is a top priority. Some students easily slip into the "teacher says, I fix" model of revising and editing. Our goal should be to help students feel empowered and able to make decisions about their own texts. Therefore, I recommend offering more than one suggestion for addressing a problem, concern, or error. When we have a suggestion to improve a text, there is always more than one way to make that revision. Give students a sense of the available options and explain why they may work. Then let students choose. The goal here is for students to realize there are multiple "right answers" in writing well.

8. *Understand the importance of end comments and of using the student's name.*

Most L2 writing scholars recommend a combination of selective margin comments and an end comment when working with ELL and multi-lingual writers (Ferris & Hedgcock, 2013, p. 198). The repetition of comments (both in the margins and at the end, as well as across essays) helps students see how the two sets of comments connect, and they can begin to recognize and find patterns within a series of instances and inac-curacies, especially when their teacher notes those patterns in the end comments.

End comments also support more global revision. Goldstein (2005) explains, "A major strength of end commentary is the ability to be sum-mative, or cumulative, thereby bringing together all of the comments in a way that educates the writer for revision of the paper as well as for future revision" (p. 90). A well-written end comment can help student writ-ers get a sense of the bigger picture—what they are doing well and how they might set goals for revision. You can also provide individualized instruction through end comments. Sometimes this is instruction that the student didn't receive during class, or it's new guidance for that par-ticular writer. Most important, end comments combined with marginal comments seem to lead to greater student understanding and learning (Kramer-Simpson, 2012).

The end comment is also an important place to personalize your feedback. Always try to use the student's name ("Dear Miguel"); point to specific positive moments in the text ("In paragraph 3, I really liked how you use that quotation from your sister" or "I liked your use of the word *XXX*. Great vocabulary and word choice decision"); and sign off with your name. For the ELLs/multilinguals in your class, these small gestures create a stronger sense of encouragement and investment, which they will need in order to keep pushing forward in their English writing. It also helps them know that you are actually reading their words and that their words matter.

9. *Use technology but be aware of its limitations.*

Like our students, we are always learning. Determining ways of provid-ing feedback is one area of teaching writing where we are always adjust-ing and improving. Sometimes the improvements are helped along by technology. I now sometimes use audio and video clips to share feedback with my students. I also like to use the Comments feature in Microsoft Word and Google Docs with students. For one, they can read these com-ments better than they can read my handwriting. Second, I go through and try to see how certain comments link together, making changes as needed for clarity. I also include hyperlinks to useful videos or webpages that may provide a good example or tutorial. I particularly like using soft-ware, such as Google Classroom and Google Docs, that allows me and the students to look at past drafts. I can get a sense of their timeline: On which days did they make the most progress? What happened that day in the classroom or in my interactions with that student?

As much as I love how technology has added new tools to my writing instruction, I'm also aware that I often have students who don't share my enthusiasm. For some, the digital divide is very real. Getting access to the Internet may be difficult for some students for any number of social and economic reasons. For instance, Miguel was frustrated when his teacher assumed he could work online from home. When the teacher had asked at the beginning of September if students in her class had Internet access, they had all said yes, even Miguel. And he was being truthful. His family did have a computer with Internet access. But his teacher had no way of knowing that Miguel had to compete for computer time with his mother, who used it to pay bills or to Skype, and with two younger siblings, who increasingly needed it to read online textbooks for their fifth- and sixth-grade homework. Plus, their apartment building had inconsistent Internet access, and there were often blocks of hours when Miguel couldn't get online to access Google or the Internet. He never told his teachers; it was embarrassing, and he didn't want them to think poorly of him or his family. Instead, many teachers questioned his homework efforts and dedication to school.

For students who have limited access to the Internet, my enthusiastic use of online comments and embedded YouTube video links will be far less helpful. It can also make students without access feel more disenfranchised. Likewise, I've grown aware that even students with regular Internet access may find the technology off-putting. Some students are more responsive to paper copies of their work with my comments than to digital copies in their Google Classroom. Quite simply, many students like shutting off the technology and feel that the teacher's handwritten note is more personal and encouraging.

In the Classroom

When Students Don't Use Feedback

One difficulty some teachers encounter is that even when they provide feedback, many ELL students are unsure what to do with it. In a recent class, Mrs. Keller provided feedback on early drafts of students' argument essays. She used the Comments feature in Google Classroom to share questions and respond to her students. As an experienced teacher of multilingual writers, Mrs. Keller followed many of the guidelines for teacher feedback outlined in the previous list. Her feedback was clear, and she asked students questions to help them expand their initial ideas and dig deeper into the meanings and detail in their arguments. She had an excellent rapport with her students, who considered her a trusted teacher. Many of them wrote back to her comments, including Adesha, a fifteen-year-old from Nepal. All seemed to be going well.

But Mrs. Keller began to notice that as much as students had acknowledged and even replied to her comments, they didn't seem to be doing anything with them. She found a few small changes in spelling or word choice, but very few students seem to be using her comments, questions, and suggestions to revise and rethink their drafts. She wondered if the students were just being polite in responding to her notes. Did they actually read her comments? Did they not understand what she was asking for? She was frustrated.

As we talked about what might be happening, we decided to ask the students. Our first question was: did you understand Mrs. Keller's comments? Again, the response was positive. As we pointed to certain comments or asked more generally about the feedback they had received, the ELL students told us: "Yes, it was a good suggestion." "The question made me think about things more deeply." "I thought it was a good idea." "Thank you for reading my essay with care." "I know I need to add more detail now." In other words, their feedback to the teacher was also positive. So why was revision not happening? Finally we asked Adesha point blank why she wasn't using Mrs. Keller's comments to revise. Her answer: "I don't know how."

Adesha's answer stunned us. Mrs. Keller's comments were clear, the suggestions we offered were clear, and students indicated they understood them. Where, then, was the disconnect? What we learned was that students couldn't fathom how to move from Mrs. Keller's comments to actual written changes on the page. They had difficulty formulating a plan and then enacting that plan. When Mrs. Keller asked them to revise, they didn't know what to do or what doing something looked like. Editing, they understood. Correct your spelling, fix that comma, fix the verb tense—these were easy enough to complete. But how to respond to a request for more detail, or a suggestion that a point might be better supported with a quote from the reading? It wasn't that students weren't listening; rather, they were grappling with the comment, striving to understand it, and unsure how to start to make those changes in their writing. When Mrs. Keller asked her class at large about what they did with her comments, many of her students, predominantly ELLs, responded as Adesha had: they had read her notes, but they had no idea how to make the kinds of changes or expansions her questions were asking for. In short, they had very little experience with revision.

We realized that more explicit teaching and discussion of how to "do revision" needed to happen. We decided to use aspects of joint construction (discussed in Chapter 4) to demonstrate some hands-on activities and teach revision. Students not only needed to see writers making revision, but they also needed to see how they did it. Once they read the teacher's comment, what came next? If they understood the comment and had some ideas for how to address the comment, then what? How did a writer come up with a plan and then implement it? From our previous work with ELLs and struggling writers more generally, we knew that for students to truly take up the craft of revision (Murray, 1995), they had to have some visceral experiences in revision. Joint construction provided us with a classroom method for exploring revision, providing tangible experiences, and opening up classroom discussions that provided a hands-on demonstration of how writers revise.

We began by asking Adesha if we could use her paper as a model. We created a large poster-size paper (24" × 36") of her draft, complete with two of Mrs. Keller's comments. Students were immediately reassured when they realized Adesha's paper had the same kinds of teacher comments that their papers had. As a class, we read aloud Adesha's essay; then we read through the first of Mrs. Keller's comments. Mrs. Keller asked students for their ideas, and again, the room went silent.

As the class began to warm up to the idea of thinking and talking through the options and Mrs. Keller's question, they eventually began to formulate suggestions for Adesha. Mrs. Keller asked two students, Janine and Shayla, to come up to the board and begin to try out the suggestions that were mentioned. Using colorful markers, Janine and Shayla began to write out ideas from the class to help Adesha expand. Students began to ask Adesha to share more details, and as she answered, a classmate would announce, "You got to add that." Janine and Shayla took notes on the board, and then checked for Adesha's approval before they added new sentences, clarifying phrases, and changed words on the large paper draft. At one point, an entirely new paragraph emerged. After dealing with the first comment, Janine and Shayla handed off the marker to Adesha, who began to take a more active role, noting that she knew what to do with this comment. She offered a rewrite, and Shayla nodded. "Yeah, that's good." Another student suggested that she might find a better word for *thing*, and then the brainstorming began again. Thirty minutes later, Mrs. Keller, with a flourish, handed Adesha her large paper draft, complete with revisions and additions and even some arrows for moving sentences around. She proudly announced to her class, "And that is how we DO revision."

As students turned their attention to their own essays, we began to see more evolution and changes across their drafts in the coming days. Adesha not only took the suggestions of her peers, but also began to revise further, drawing on a renewed sense of confidence and purpose.

Often, we ask second language and novice writers to complete aspects of the writing process, but we give them few strategies and chances to try them out in safe ways. This is especially true when it comes to revision.

Many teachers and students spend little time demonstrating strategies and enacting hands-on techniques that illustrate how to work with feedback and how to revise. These are skills that often feel invisible to ELLs and multilingual writers, and they can find it challenging to develop and deepen their writing. If students are expected to learn how to expand and improve on their drafts, we need to dedicate time in the classroom to show them how. Digging deep into one's writing and developing critical thinking skills related to planning and implementing changes is an important part of the writing process.

Mrs. Keller found that she had to do this Big Paper revision activity a few times over the course of the year. Even as her students gained more experience as writers, there were moments later in the semester when they simply stalled out during revision. Sometimes they were thrown off because they were working with a new genre or writing for a new audience, and they felt frozen by what they perceived as new obstacles in writing. They would stop responding to teacher comments and made few changes across drafts. At other times, Mrs. Keller noted that she seemed to be making the same comments again and again for the same students. We learned to be patient, and we also found that repetition—repetitive comments with similar suggestions—could actually be part of the learning cycle for some students.

Improving Accuracy: Rethinking Approaches to Error Correction

In recent years, I've started to change the language I use to talk about errors with ELLs/multilinguals. Instead of error, I talk about improving accuracy, drawing on terms used by Ferris and Hedgcock (2013). I like this terminology because it seems to encourage and build confidence in student writers. The term *error* tends to feed into deficit models of writing and discourages students who struggle, whereas the phrase "improving accuracy" reflects a goal of helping all of our students improve their writing. The notion of improving accuracy can be applied on a number of levels. It can mean improving descriptions, offering more evidence, or adding detail. It can mean paying more attention to transitions within or across paragraphs. It can mean indenting paragraphs, improving word choices, adjusting verb tenses, and using commas with care. When I work with ELL writers, I often compare improving accuracy in writing to trying to shoot an arrow at a bull's-eye. Sometimes students may be a bit off target, but with each paper and new writing situation, they should be aiming to get closer to that bull's-eye. And it takes practice. Olympic archers take hundreds, if not thousands, of shots. Even the best of them can get nervous and miss the target when shooting in a new arena or new event—the same way that a writer can make more errors if he or she is faced with a new genre, a new audience, or an unfamiliar topic.

Overall, the concept of improving accuracy helps move the teacher-student conversations and student thinking about writing beyond "just fixing it," and it encourages students to think about why certain changes and edits may be helpful for readers.

One Size Doesn't Fit All

No single type of error is common to all ELL writers. Each student writer is an individual, and each student will have different areas in which he or she needs to improve accuracy. In general, though, teachers may find that ELL students have difficulties with some of the following (Ferris, 2006):

- Verb tense
- Passive constructions
- Subject-verb agreement
- Formation of tenses/verb forms
- Count/non-count nouns
- Plural and possessive noun endings
- Use of articles

- Word order
- Word choice
- Punctuation
- Spelling
- Idioms
- Sentence structure

So What Should Teachers Do?

My advice here repeats an earlier recommendation: be selective. Teachers should look for patterns of error and offer suggestions for how the student might correct or address the concern. Ideally, offer one to two suggestions for improved accuracy, and try to explain why the error is a problem for readers. For example, if the error is related to the incorrect or inconsistent use of past tense in verbs, it may be helpful to explain how verb tense provides readers with a sense of when an action took place in time. For readers, the understanding of time helps them know how to place a particular moment or action the writer is describing.

When teachers notice a particular pattern of error, the next step is to describe the error from a functional and rhetorical perspective. Stating the rule is helpful, but if a teacher can articulate how that rule matters to or helps readers, then it's more likely to resonate with student writers. Some teachers feel a bit uneasy about this aspect of feedback. Many monolingual, native speakers of English know when something isn't right, but they have a more difficult time articulating *why* it isn't right or how that rule came to be. It can be helpful for teachers to develop a stronger sense of linguistics, rhetorical grammar, and the history of the English language in order to be able to offer students more precise explanations. Many teacher education and writing teacher programs are now encouraging new teachers to take a few classes in TESOL or linguistics to strengthen their understanding of linguistic patterns and usage.

The Use of Accuracy Logs

One goal of improving accuracy should be to help students develop the skills to become more independent. Accuracy logs, sometimes called "error logs," offer one concrete strategy for helping students become stronger readers of their own work, with the guidance of their teachers (see Figure 5.1). Accuracy logs are often set up by teachers and then continued by the individual student. The log catalogs an error, explains why it is an error, along with the rule, and then includes two possible example solutions. With each subsequent writing assignment, the teacher requests that the student use his or her error log to try to identify similar errors and then make changes to address the error, based on the suggestions in the log. As the year goes on, the log may lengthen as teachers add new areas to consider. Students develop a kind of checklist to help them correct and identify specific concerns in their own writing.

When I work with ELL writers, I often stress that I have an internal accuracy log. In all honesty, there are a few errors and stylistic problems that I tend to repeat in my writing. For example, I always struggle to spell *separate*, and I know when I get excited about a particular topic, I can sometimes repeat certain phras-

Figure 5.1. Sample of an accuracy log.

Student Name:		Teacher:	
Accuracy Log			
Date/ Assignment	Error type (name of error and an example from student's writing)	Possible correction and/or sample correct examples	Self-correct (for student's use in next draft/assignment) check box. (√)

ing. Over the years, I've learned that it's not always a good idea to interrupt my writing to correct all these concerns as I'm trying to compose. But these repetitions, spelling concerns, and other idiosyncrasies of my writing are things I need to look for when I revise and correct for accuracy in order to make my work more effective and more enjoyable for readers.

In the Classroom

Samuel and the Problem of Sentence Boundaries

Last year, I worked with seventeen-year-old Samuel, who recently emigrated from Haiti. Samuel rushed into his writing with enthusiasm, especially when he was excited about his topic. He loved writing narratives and personal memoirs about his experiences living through the 2010 earthquake. His depictions contained powerful imagery of his mother sheltering him and heartbreaking depictions of lost children, death, and crumbling concrete.

But when Samuel wrote sentences, he often forgot to capitalize the first letter. He also often forgot end punctuation, layering one thought on top of the other as his ideas flowed onto the page. (Samuel is not alone in this practice. Learning to identify sentence boundaries is a common problem for some English language learners, especially those who come from language backgrounds that have different customs and rules for sentence boundaries.) As Samuel and I worked side by side to revise his narratives, I spoke to him about why sentence boundaries were important for readers. Samuel knew the rules, but when he wrote he often was typing rather quickly. Stopping for end punctuation and reaching for the SHIFT key that would change a letter to a capital felt to him as if it would slow him down.

For my part, as I watched him generate beautiful and rich material about his homeland and his mother, I could understand his fears about slowing down. I didn't want him to slow down either. But the end result of his drafting was a narrative that was difficult to read, mostly because I struggled to place it into the chunks I was accustomed to as a reader.

As I worked with Samuel, I began by reviewing the rules. "What do you need to start a sentence?"

"Oh, yeah. A capital. I forgot."

"Great. But let's look at this one. Can you tell me where this sentence ends?"

"Umm [reads the sentences on the page] . . . here. I think I need a period there."

"Yes, perfect place. You know the rules."

"Yeah, I just never do them."

Rather than reviewing the rule again or handing him a worksheet, I started talking with Samuel about sentences. Why do readers need sentences? Why happens when a reader encounters a narrative without punctuation? I asked him to start reading his own narrative, but to try to imagine that he was a reader who wasn't familiar with the story or the mother described on the page. As Samuel read, he noted that readers would probably be confused because all the words seemed to run together. I asked him how such readers might feel when trying to read his work, noting that it was a powerful narrative. Samuel said, "I think it might make their heads hurt. A headache. You know?"

This conversation provided a perfect opportunity for me to mention to Samuel how our brains like to "chunk" information to help us process it. Sentences help us understand where to start and where to end. Capital letters and end punctuation such as periods, exclamation marks, and questions marks help readers know those "starting" and "end" points. They help us to chunk, and in doing so, they help us to read.

Other kinds of punctuation help us to sort out relationships between words and pieces of information. Samuel then asked if this is why teachers like paragraphs. He didn't often use paragraphs in his longer pieces. "I don't understand the rules."

Samuel had completed many worksheets and sat through many lectures on the rules, but the logic of the rules was never discussed in ways that made sense to him. All the rules felt somewhat random. But when we started talking about how these conventions helped readers understand sentences or texts or even the writer's intentions more clearly, Samuel became more invested in looking at his paper more closely. He would spend the next two days coming voluntarily to the classroom after school, two hours in total, working quietly at a desk adding punctuation to his narrative, figuring out those starts and endings—one line at a time. The work was labor-intensive and often frustrating, but Samuel, of his own volition, stayed with it. This piece was worth his time, and he wanted to make sure readers could understand it.

Navigating Peer Review in a Linguistically Diverse Classroom

When I've taught college-level writers over the past few years, I've always asked about their past experiences with peer review. The conversation that ensues is always a bit of a mixed bag. Some student writers report that peer review in high school was "a waste of time." Others say they never really did it well because they hated sharing their work with their peers, even those who were their friends. Some report that if they were lucky, someone in their group would correct all their spelling and grammar mistakes. But every year, and in every writing class, there are always a few students who talk about experiences in peer review that made them better writers, stronger readers of their friends' papers, and more knowledgeable about writing in general. They began to feel more confident about what they saw working in a piece of writing and better at identifying what wasn't. When I hear these students' voices, I am always challenged to dig a bit deeper. What worked for these students that didn't work for others? Universally students tell me that three things made the difference: the teacher, a supportive—and safe—class environment, and a strong sense of protocol around peer review.

Teachers face some unique considerations when peer interaction includes ELL/multilingual student writers. Studies have also found that in mixed classrooms, ELL writers can be at a disadvantage with monolingual, native English speakers, particularly regarding oral responses in a small group setting. Zhu (2001), for example, found that ELL/multilingual writers were often silenced, interrupted, and generally pushed to the outskirts of the conversation. Once interrupted, they often gave up their turn and didn't finish making their comments, even when they were on the verge of making a good point to the writer. These students are required to write and formulate a response in a language they are often still learning to master.

Some ELL/multilingual students see some benefits in peer review and enjoy the social aspects of those classroom interactions. But others hate peer review sessions in their ELA class, often "forgetting" copies of their papers for those sessions, even when the papers are diligently present in their binders. ELL writers may also be less direct in their feedback than their peers; their strategy may be to announce and clarify what they have read, or to ask questions. They imply or suggest changes rather than insist on them. Sometimes ELL writers are hesitant to contribute at all, feeling as though they have limited authority. Students report that they feel uncomfortable correcting other students' work when they are not yet confident in their own English writing skills. In addition, ELL writers are navigating across different communicative expectations and deciphering different attitudes about group work in the classroom.

It is important for teachers to understand that for adolescent ELL writers, peer review is a particularly risky task. Imagine that all your flaws in written language, as well as all your flaws in oral language, are at the center of a small-group discussion with peers you may or may not know very well. Or you have been asked to read and respond to a monolingual English student's paper, and you feel that everyone in the room knows that English is not your first language. You worry that they will question your judgments. You worry that you might just be wrong in your advice. What do you know, after all? Even for native English speakers, the whole process can make you feel like you never really owned English at all. Studies tell us that in mixed peer review groups, monolingual English speakers often disregard the input and advice of their multilingual peers, even when that advice is well articulated and accurate. ELL and multilingual writers are often interrupted before they can finish their suggestions. Some ELL writers simply shut down in these situations and disengage, with a quiet murmur of "yeah, it's really good." In some situations, monolingual English speakers feel that their "job" in the group is to tutor multilingual writers and often (falsely) assume there is nothing they can learn about writing from the ELL writers in the group.

Embracing the Teacher's Role in a Mixed Peer Review

The most productive peer review sessions come out of an acknowledgment that writers don't just "do peer review" to complete a step of a four- or five-step regimented writing process. As writing teachers, we use peer review because we are trying to teach students how to think through and develop ideas about how to write, read, and respond to texts. There are real, concrete curricular objectives we need to do a better job of articulating to ourselves, our colleagues, and our students. If we begin to see peer review as part of our teachable goals—part of the learning objectives for our classrooms—it then becomes easier to see that we need to teach students how to "do review."

Preparing all students for peer review is the necessary component to building a productive peer review model in the writing classroom. In my experience, all students—ELLs/multilinguals and monolinguals, at all academic levels—need training to do peer review well. As a teacher, I do a good deal of behind the scenes work to ensure more productive sessions. Here are some ideas for preparing students.

Setting the Stage

- Openly discuss turn-taking strategies for peer review with the whole class. Suggest procedures to level the playing field for all student reviewers.
- Teach students to recognize the differences between good peer review and

bad peer review. One idea that can help accomplish this is a "fishbowl" technique, in which the class watches as fellow students act out a good example of a peer response session and a poor example. After the enactments, students discuss as a class what worked and what didn't for both the writer and the reviewer in the fishbowl demonstration. Students respond well to seeing a peer review session "gone wrong" and then working as a class to identify exactly what went wrong and what might have worked better.

- Use the demonstration as a way to set classroom goals and guidelines for peer review. Videos of peer review sessions are also useful, and many examples from college writing centers can now be found online through YouTube.

- Clearly explain the responsibilities of readers and writers. Often writers feel as though they have no responsibility or that they are just passive listeners in the peer review session. Encourage writers to see their roles as more active.

  o **The writer.** When student writers come to peer review workshop, they should always have a reason for being there. They should have questions about their work or about ways to approach the writing process, they want to be able to set their own agenda for writing help, or they just want an audience for their work. Encourage student writers to prepare for peer review by being ready with the following: (1) questions, (2) a current draft, outline, notes, etc., and (3) a copy of the assignment sheet.

  o **The "underprepared writer."** Even if the student writer is not prepared (e.g., hasn't completed the assignment, has an incomplete draft, etc.), readers can still help, whether by clarifying goals, finding out what the writer wants to do, or helping to brainstorm thesis topics. The student can also provide support to other writers in the group. There is no reason to exempt a student writer from a peer response session, even if he or she isn't prepared. The teacher can also start peer review by asking writers to identify three questions (or areas of concern), which they write down and then share with their peer groups before they start to discuss a given paper.

  o **The reader.** Remind students that in their roles as readers, their primary responsibility is not to merely improve a writer's grade (though that's nice too!), but to leave each writer with something that will remain useful long after the end of the session.

- Hold a class discussion in which you and the students discuss useful vocabulary for participating in peer response. Provide some models, and create a word wall with those cues posted for all students to refer to. This is also an excellent way to increase the academic language and vocabulary of ELL/multilingual students.

Behind the scenes:

- Take an active role in creating student review groups. You know the personalities and strengths of your students well. Put that knowledge to use when you create the groups. Limit each group to three of four students, and strategically bring together students with different strengths and mutually beneficial styles of response.

- Assign roles to each student in a peer review groups to ensure that everyone is participating and to provide a clear structure for the group work. Roles might include timekeeper, note-taker, writer, solicitor of comments (Liu & Hansen, 2002).

- Allow students to read the papers the day before so that time in class can be used solely for responding. If that isn't possible, try to structure time in productive ways.

- Allow ELL/L2 writers to use their L1 when they take notes.

Switch it up:

- Try not to rely on only one form of peer response. Indeed, it's helpful for ELL/multilingual students to have a sense of familiarity with the peer review process; familiarity breeds confidence, and it can help students concentrate on gaining their skills as readers and reviewers. But after a while, all students can get bored, and peer review can become less effective.

- Switch it up, in terms of both groups and methods. Although many L2 writers are most comfortable with the oral aspects of peer response, it's useful to create opportunities for written feedback. Having students learn to write peer response letters is one such idea.

Ultimately, peer review, whether in a classroom or through a high school writing center, is a valuable way for teachers to build a feedback cycle that provides student writers with more than one reader—someone beyond "just the teacher." Peer review, when it is taught explicitly and done well, builds the reading, critical thinking, and communicative skills of all students. It encourages students to become close and insightful readers of texts. They learn to consider not only the editorial and mechanical aspects of the writer's texts, but also how the text is going to be perceived, understood, and used by other readers, both monolingual and multilingual. In peer review, students learn to think about how effectively a regular text—from a peer, not from a textbook or a published author—achieves its purpose, and they learn to strategize the ways a text can be improved. From a communicative standpoint, peer review encourages students to learn how to give and how to receive critique, praise, and suggestions in ways that don't alienate the writer, but instead encourage them to press on. These are not easy communicative or social skills to learn, but they are an essential part of workplace and civic engagement.

Consideration for ELL/Multilingual Writers

Some ELL/multilingual students will be well prepared for the task of peer review, and for many, setting some clear examples and expectations for good review, along with some training for the entire class, will help boost their confidence and help them to become more active participants. But you may also have some ELL/multilingual writers who are still struggling with listening, reading, or speaking skills. For those students, here are some additional recommendations:

- Consider using a written mode of peer response first. In oral sessions, allow students to record the discussion so that they can listen again on their own, or choose a person to be the note-taker for the group and make copies of those notes for all students in the group.

- Give students their peers' papers a day earlier to allow them time to write out their comments. Some students may be unsure about articulating their feedback; they may also worry about pronunciation or misspeaking. In those situations, provide students with sample response letters. Also provide students with sample phrases or helpful terms they can turn to during peer review sessions.

- If students have difficulties with reading, provide papers earlier and consider having all students read their paper aloud as other students follow along on copies.

- Group students by the content area or by similar subjects. Then allow students to meet before their first drafts to share background information on their topics. This technique helps all participants develop schemata for reading and talking about the papers during peer review.

Moving from Response to Assessment

This chapter has provided insights into how teachers working with linguistically and culturally diverse student writers can provide the best kinds of feedback to those writers to encourage growth, confidence, and future success in writing well. Teacher response, corrections, and assessments are crucial parts of a writing teacher's work, but they must ultimately be seen as part of the greater teaching and learning cycle that surrounds each writing assignment and the teacher's overall course goals. In many ways, the aspects of feedback and even of the SFL teaching-learning cycle provide teachers with ample opportunities to give formative feedback and to conduct formative assessments. In the next chapter, I take up summative assessment, grading, classroom evaluation, and large-scale assessment in order to consider how teachers might answer questions about "what is fair?" and "how do I grade my ELL/multilingual writers and their texts?"

Chapter Six

Appropriate and Equitable: Thoughts on Evaluation and Grading

Those who deal with ESL writers must evaluate their writing fairly, in both mass and classroom testing contexts. They need to understand that second language acquisition is a slow and gradual process and that expecting ESL students' writing to be indistinguishable in terms of grammar from that of their NES counterparts is naive and unrealistic. Teachers also need to recognize that ESL writers' rhetorical differences may be manifestations of their cultural backgrounds and not cognitive or educational deficiencies. Testers need to provide writing prompts and contexts that do not disadvantage ESL students. Finally, it is important to understand that acceptable performance in one's classes (including writing classes) means more than the results of any writing test, no matter how well constructed.

— Tony Silva, "On the Ethical Treatment of ESL Writers"

In this chapter, I want to share some ideas for developing fair, equitable, and formative guidelines for grading the written work of ELL and multilingual writers. Many teachers struggle with how to approach grading the work of students who are still trying to master English. Here, I address the concerns about evaluation from a few different angles: large-scale assessment, classroom assessment, student self-assessment and reflection, and the positive and negative ways that our assessment practices "wash back" into our curriculum and impact our instruction.

Large-Scale Assessments

Let me begin by discussing some of the large-scale assessments that English language learners, or students with limited English proficiency (LEP), already participate in through public school districts. Upon arriving in most school districts, most students who are identified as speaking a language other than English in the home are tested for English language proficiency. Some multilingual students will pass this test with flying colors. Another language may be spoken in the home, but these students are also beautifully proficient in English as well. This initial testing may also identify students who are still in need of English language development tutoring or coursework. Despite the results of these tests, parents can, and sometimes do, decide to opt their children out of ELL services.

The results of these assessments have an impact on students and schools. Some students may receive limited services—a few hours a week—of homework help or take a specific class on academic language, reading, or writing. This initial assessment also helps ELL professionals, often in conversation with parents, guardians, and even students, to decide what the best course options are for the individual student. In districts with large populations of ELLs, this assessment may also determine placement within a larger ELL program that has multiple tiers of EL classes.

In addition to this initial screening, students formally identified as ELL must take annual English language proficiency exams, which test oral proficiency, listening, reading, and writing. In my home state of New Hampshire, we are part of the WIDA Consortium, a consortium of more than seventeen states that provides support for advancing the academic language development of linguistically diverse students. WIDA also provides an assessment test, called the ACCESS test, which helps ELL teachers and their schools track the proficiency levels and improvements of these English learners each year, until they are exited from the ELL program in their schools or districts. Upon exiting, many students remain on "monitor status," meaning that an ELL teacher or administrator continues to check on how students are performing.

I share this information for two reasons: (1) ELL students already encounter multiple assessments beyond those that monolingual students encounter, and (2) ELL teachers may have important information to share with content area teachers about the strengths and challenges individual ELL writers face. For example, the WIDA Consortium has its own established standards for English language development that identify performance definitions for writing, as well as speaking and reading. These performance definitions emphasize guiding principles for language development, age-appropriate academic language, and model performance indicators, all available by grade level clusters. In the WIDA standards, performance indicators are defined as: Entering, Beginning, Developing, Expanding, and Bridging.

Content area teachers may find it beneficial to ask ELL teaching colleagues about the standards and assessment tests used by their schools and districts. Teachers may also find it useful to examine how ELL standards overlap with ELA frameworks and standards used by their districts. For example, I encourage pre-service ELA teachers to look at the state standards for ELA alongside the WIDA standards, with a particular focus on Expanding and Bridging performance indicators, which are often for students who are placed in "mainstream" ELA classrooms. This activity helps these future teachers have a better understanding of the kinds of preparation ELLs may have already had, and it also puts them on the first step toward better communication and sharing with the ELL teachers in their future schools.

In this age of assessments and standards, English teachers are aware that many of their linguistically diverse students will also have to perform on statewide assessments such as the PARCC or Smarter Balanced exams, both tied to the Common Core State Standards Initiative, or on state-developed tests. While multiple arguments can be made for and against these assessments, a major concern is that these kinds of tests are not often normed with linguistically diverse students in mind and too often contain questions that are culturally biased. In recent years, there has been a more concerted effort to include L2 writing specialists in the discussions around exam production held by the companies and groups that manufacture these tests. But, as with all testing, concerns remain.

These large-scale exams impact classroom practice in significant ways—particularly because concern for the exams leads teachers to limit the kinds of writing experiences and instruction they provide to ELL and multilingual writers.

Classroom Assessment

Beyond the school-wide assessments that teachers encounter, there are the daily and weekly assessments that teachers must contend with—that stack of papers on the end of the desk. The challenge of assessing student writing is one that most teachers—especially English teachers—find familiar. When is an A an A? What role should effort or revision play in the final grade? How can I be sure my grading is fair? What about rubrics? When it comes to grading the written work of students writing in a second or third language, these questions become even more complicated. Certain evaluation practices are decidedly unfair. For example, a college professor I knew told students he would stop reading (and grading) if he encountered more than three errors on the opening page of a student's paper. As a college student, I had a professor who announced he would mark off five points for every error on the page. Six errors would start a student at a C-, regardless of research, innovative ideas, and quality of content. As a student writer, such evaluation procedures were terrifying and, while on some level they forced me to be attentive to proofreading and correction, they also made me and other students fear writing. Imagine for a moment what these kinds of grading protocols can mean for students writing in a second language. For second language writers, these approaches are not only excruciating, but they also create situations that lead to failure with writing and create a counterproductive environment that makes ELL writers less engaged and less confident.

Toward More Equitable Grading Protocols

> ESL students can become very fluent writers of English, but they may never become indistinguishable from a native speaker, and it is not clear why they should.
> —Ilona Leki (1992b, p. 132)

> Given the cognitive demands of reading and writing in a second language, along with the inevitability of what we may see as written accent in L2 writing, it should be fair to assess L2 students differently in comparison to their L1 peers, by extending deadlines, adjusting page-length requirements, not being as particular about SWE [Standard Written English]."
> —Michelle Cox and Terry Myers Zawacki [2015, p. 22]

As these quotations suggest, many ELL and multilingual writers will continue to have traces of "written accent" in their English writing. Furthermore, ELL and multilingual writers will spend more time and more cognitive energy generating and revising their written texts than monolingual, native English speakers. Writing in a second or third language is simply more demanding on multiple levels. I'm often reminded of the dancers Fred Astaire and Ginger Rogers when I think about grading the papers of ELL students. Over the years, many have questioned why Fred Astaire is perceived as the consummate professional dancer, while Ginger Rogers is often viewed simply as his partner. After all, Ginger Rogers performed all the moves Fred Astaire did—but backwards and in high heels—yet didn't get the same salary, recognition, or adoration. I think of ELL and multilingual writers in ELA classrooms as the overlooked and underappreciated Ginger Rogers of writing. They are working in a second language, reading and revising in that language, and often mired in time constraints and expectations that focus negatively on differences, not on innovations and positives.

But grading students is also an essential aspect of teaching and learning, so it's imperative to find ways to acknowledge and appreciate the differences, while at the same time offering students evaluative feedback that helps them learn. As Ken

Hyland explains, "Without information gained from assessments it would be difficult to identify the gaps between students' current and target performances and to help them progress" (2003, p. 212).

General Recommendations for Responsive and Equitable Assessment Practices

- Provide students with an overview of the goals and learning outcomes for each major writing assignment. Review these goals, along with the goals for the particular genre, at multiple points throughout the teaching cycle (e.g., during deconstruction, during joint construction, during the individual construction phases, discussed in Chapter 4).

- Be explicit about your criteria and evaluate with those criteria in mind.

- Use deconstruction of model texts and peer review to help students become better equipped to identify and evaluate what is working in a piece of writing and what is not.

- Consider ways to incorporate student self-reflection and self-assessment in the evaluation process.

- Have students keep a portfolio of their writing so that both you and your students can consider progress through comparison across various assignments.

- Provide students with feedback that notes their progress and success, as well as what they need to work toward in future assignments.

Recognizing the Strengths and Weaknesses of Rubrics

Rubrics are important tools for writing teachers. They help us to reflect and consider our goals for instruction and our goals for student outcomes. They help teachers stay on track with their assessment—to be fair—as they read across a large volume of student work. They help teachers to identify and articulate the qualities that make a piece of writing successful. For many students, the rubric provides a way for them to see what a teacher values in a written text, in the writing process, in a specific genre, or in the development of ideas. When teachers share rubrics with their students, many ELL and multilingual writers appreciate knowing what the teacher is looking for and how they might achieve a certain targeted grade.

But rubrics also have weaknesses (Wilson, 2006, 2007). As teachers know, rubrics often box us into seeing only certain qualities and not others. Rubrics can limit what students imagine or strive for in their written work. Furthermore, these days many of the rubrics teachers use are taken from websites, from district purchases of large-scale writing instruction programs, and from assessment tests. For teachers working with linguistically diverse classrooms, it's important to realize that most of these prepackaged rubrics have not been normed with or even considered students writing in a second language. And if they are normed, they are built around the assumption that all student writers are monolingual English speakers.

Even if some rubric categories seem to allow for the creativity and differences or innovations that multilingual writers bring to their texts—such as voice—school-wide initiatives can intentionally or unintentionally devalue the aspects of rubrics that multilingual writers tend to do well in. For example, I was recently in a seventh-grade ELA classroom where the teacher explicitly told parents that the team had decided to double the value points for organization and mechanics for the upcoming year and drop the category of voice from the school's rubric. There was concern that voice wasn't evaluated highly on the state-mandated tests. Let's consider this shift from a second language writing perspective. For one, many teachers find that second language writers, with their diverse experiences, language practices, and cultural resources, often bring a great deal of voice and innovation to their written texts. When voice is devalued in or erased from rubrics, we devalue what many ELL writers do well. Furthermore, we can question what a rubric values in terms of organization. As I've mentioned in earlier chapters, organization of genres and texts is often culturally influenced. Rubrics that consider organization do not often define the term in culturally inclusive ways, and multilingual students lose points for incorporating organizational patterns that may be effective but follow different cultural norms.

To counter these concerns, teachers should try to develop local rubrics, based on their students, their goals for student outcomes, the genre and audience, and the goals of instruction. The most powerful rubrics are often those designed collaboratively by the teacher with the class, as the students help to articulate the goals and outcomes of a particular genre and writing assignment. I also recommend that teachers consider adding a category for what I've started calling "innovations." An innovations category allows teachers to acknowledge creative phrasing, the effective use of a student's first language incorporated into the text, an interesting and illustrative comparison, or a particularly perceptive communicative insight into a genre or an audience.

Teachers can also develop (or build on) multiple-trait grading strategies that evaluate students' understanding of specific genre features and the communicative aspects of writing. Rubrics for writing assignments can include criteria for participation in deconstructions and joint constructions, multiple drafts and revision efforts, awareness of reader/writer context, sense of purpose and task, cooperative interactions, content, and self-reflection (Hamp-Lyons & Condon, 2000, p. 144).

Student Self-Assessment: Building Skills in Metacognition and Meta-Awareness

Teachers should try to create mandatory opportunities for student self-reflection in their grading procedures. I often ask students to compose a cover letter to me for each major writing assignment. For that task, I ask them to share the history of their papers and how the papers unfolded for them as writers. I ask about the parts they are most proud of, but also about the challenges. I encourage them to think about these strengths and challenges, not only in terms of written texts, but also in terms of process, their learning and development as writers, and the ways in which they drew on their strengths.

By adding opportunities for self-reflection to the writing process, I hope to help students become stronger readers of their own work. One way to get started is by practicing and learning how to be good peer reviewers (as discussed in Chapter 5). In learning how to review and respond to the texts of their peers, student writers also become better readers of their own work. They learn what to look for, can begin to identify their own weaknesses and strengths, and are better prepared to read their work with a more critical eye toward improvement and revision. But none of these valuable skills happens overnight, and none of these skills appears without the guiding hand of the teacher.

The accuracy logs, mentioned in Chapter 5, are another way to help students develop the skills to become more careful readers of their own work. Again, this kind of work takes time, and it's important to remember how time-consuming and challenging it can be to write in a second language. But if students are given the time and engaging opportunities to work as writers, they will rise to the challenge.

Students also need to develop metacognitive understandings of how texts and writers work. Therefore, I try to develop moments in my lesson planning in which students can read and evaluate their own work and writing process at various moments in the teaching-learning cycle of an assignment. For example, as students work on their own writing assignments, teachers might ask them to do a quickwrite on the readers they are writing for, asking them to consider those readers' expectations or what might make them interested in the writing. At another point, teachers might ask students to write for a few moments about the challenges or obstacles they are encountering and then try to problem-solve with the teacher or in small groups. At the end of every major writing assignment, teachers should consider having students write up either a short history of how the paper evolved over time, or what they might want to change if they had more time.

A similar type of reflective piece might be a "Where to Go from Here" free-write in which students identify not only what went well with their final drafts, but also what they might want to improve in their next writing assignment. Sometimes these areas of improvement are pragmatic and language based: "I want to improve my spelling." "I wish I had included more details around this particular scene." But I also encourage my students to think about how they might improve the *conditions* around their writing: "Next time, I want to start earlier" or "I think I do better writing at home, so next time, I'm going to try to work on my writing outside of school as well" or "Next time, I think I might listen more to my peers during peer review."

I also ask students to write about the goals of the assignment and how achieving those goals prepares them for writing in the future. My objective is to create moments that help them realize how the writing they are doing in my class is preparing them for future assignments and also for future writing situations outside of the classroom. The aim in these discussions and reflective writing prompts is to help build a stronger sense of transfer as students move from one writing situation (or classroom) to the next. For ELL writers, I don't use all of these reflective prompts at once, instead choosing those that may be most effective at a particular point in the school year. I am constantly led by the knowledge that ELL/multilingual writers are intelligent communicators and that my goal is to continually encourage and develop confidence in their writing lives.

Using Journals and Word Counts

I often encourage teachers to have their students keep reflective journals throughout the academic year. These journals serve a number of purposes. They can be used for brainstorming, for following up on a classroom discussion, for deconstructing a model text with a peer, or even for reflections at any point in the SFL writing process or when students are composing their essays.

When I first recommended using journals, the students I worked with often wrote quickly and then shoved their journals to the side. Their entries were often simple one- to two-line sentences, if I was lucky. Their reluctance and sometimes fear of writing was visible.

To begin to help students work on developing stamina in their writing, I suggested "writing targets" for each student. (Some teachers already use similar strategies to raise reading levels, encouraging students to read a certain number of words or pages each week. Since reading and writing skills are interconnected [Hirvela, 2004], reading targets are another great idea for ELLs/multilinguals.)

In developing writing targets, teachers create individualized word count goals for students' journal entries. In practice, at certain times of the year, I suggested to students that we turn these writing targets into a contest of sorts, complete with a word count chart on the wall. If the class members met their target word count numbers, we would have a pizza party or no homework. Students who made great individual progress (seven to twenty-five words, for instance, from one journal entry to the next) got prizes or a shout-out in class. Overall, the goal was not to use the journals as a punishment, but to find ways to encourage more writing, particularly more low-stakes writing, to help them gain more comfort with writing. Students could even switch back and forth between their first language and English if they got stuck in any way. These journals were not graded on grammar, and generally my comments were sparse but encouraging. The outcome was always directed toward the goal of listening to students' ideas and encouraging more words.

The journals and keeping track of individual students' word counts also proved useful for other teachers. As one teacher explained to me, it was easy to lose track of how much her students were actually writing in a given week. In any given month or academic year, there were weeks when testing—or even reading a novel—seemed to take precedence in the classroom. Students could unintentionally go for days and even weeks without writing. The teacher sometimes didn't notice, and students rarely complained. There was so much to accomplish in a given week. When I mentioned the journals and word count walls, the teacher took me up on the idea. She noted that having students keep journals and track their word counts also served as a reminder to her of how little or how much students were writing that week. As she explained, "It kept me honest about the amount of writing students were actually doing or not doing." It reminded her how easily writing could slip to the background of her teaching and how that loss of writing time affected her students' confidence and stamina in creating texts and getting their words onto the page.

Positive and Negative Washback: How Assessment Impacts Curriculum and Instruction

Research, including my own, has illustrated how testing mandates impact curricular and writing opportunities for ELL/multilingual writers, often trapping them in a curriculum that emphasizes what I've come to call "survival genres" (Enright, 2011; Enright & Gilliland, 2011; Ortmeier-Hooper, 2013) and test-based activities. Sara C. Weigle (2002) and Deborah Crusan (2010), L2 writing specialists who have written extensively on assessment, describe what they term assessment *washback*, the ways in which how and what we assess "washes" backwards into what and how we teach. Weigle explains that our assessment procedures and tools (both state-wide and classroom based) can have "positive washback" on our instructional practices, meaning that we have meaningful assessments that lead to meaningful and engaged teaching practices and student writing experiences. Or we can have "negative washback," in which assessments limit the kinds of genres we teach, lead to less engaged writing experiences for students, and constrict the ways in which we deliver instruction. As teachers, we should always be analyzing assessments—our own and those given to our students by others—with a critical eye toward how those assessments are influencing and washing back onto our teaching methods, our assignments, and our student writers, particularly our ELL/multilingual students.

We need to be asking: In what ways has testing limited the kinds of writing I allow my students to experience? In what ways do the tests limit the genres and forms that my students see and write? What do they need to know beyond the tests, and how can I create formative and summative assessment practices that create opportunities for expansion, creativity, and student investment in their work as writers? How can my assessment practices encourage my students and me to value the strengths of multilingual English speakers? How can my assessment procedures, along with my assignments and instructional methods, encourage ELL/ multilingual students to see writing as a way to have an impact on their communities, their personal lives, and the broader world? In the final chapter, I take up this critical issue by exploring social justice and transformation, and I begin to offer some ways for ELA teachers to embrace their work with these writers beyond the classroom.

Chapter Seven

Creating a School Culture That Supports Multilingual Writers

Teachers working to better meet the needs of linguistically diverse students need support. NCTE encourages English teachers to collaborate and work closely with ESL and bilingual teaching professionals, who can offer classroom support, instructional advice, and general insights into second language acquisition. School administrators should support and encourage teachers to attend workshops and professional conferences that regularly offer sessions on bilingual learners, particularly in the areas of reading and writing. Schools should also consider seeking professional development for their teachers from neighboring colleges. In turn, colleges and universities providing teacher education should offer all preservice teachers, as well as teachers pursuing advanced degree work, preparation in teaching linguistically diverse learners in their future classrooms. Coursework should be offered on second language writing and reading, and on second language acquisition, as well as on culture, and should be encouraged for all teachers.

    —NCTE Position Paper on the Role of English Teachers
       in Educating English Language Learners (ELLs)

Throughout this book, I have considered what we know about writing in a second language, and I have focused on responding to ELL writers, on building culturally responsive writing assignments, on assessment, and on concrete strategies for teaching writing in diverse classrooms. If you have this book in your hands, you are most likely a teacher who is committed to teaching all the students in your classroom. In this final chapter, my goals are twofold: (1) to begin to consider how the ways in which we teach writing are linked to social justice, and (2) to consider how we might use our talents and interests in the extracurricular aspects of our schools to create more opportunities for our ELL/multilingual writers.

Social Justice and the Teaching of Writing

> We must focus on social justice and equity as key aspects of a vision of teaching and learning to improve the preparation of teachers to work with students of color, low-income students, and ELLs.
>
> —Luciana de Oliveira (2013, p. 2)

In the movies, we have images and stories that illustrate how teaching writing can be part of a social movement or a chance to create new opportunities for young people. Films such as *Dead Poets Society*, *Dangerous Minds*, and *Freedom Writers* come to mind. Idealistic portraits all of them—but still, they inspire. And they also remind us of the power that students can develop and the agency they can find through their written texts.

As I enter my twentieth year as a teacher of writing, I've come more and more to think about how writing well is closely tied to issues of social justice and access for so many youth in the United States. This is particularly true of multilingual and ELL students. The divide that is constructed between nonnative and native speakers of English continues to erode internationally, but within the United States, English has increasingly been used as one way to distinguish what some see as "insiders" from "outsiders." It's a dividing line that I witnessed often as the daughter of immigrant parents. My mother, who spoke English well but with a heavy German accent, was disregarded at department store counters. In her younger years, I would watch in awe as she stared down those who would question her claim to the American dream, her hard work, and her status as an immigrant, and then citizen. She fought to make sure that her children would not be questioned in the same ways, while ensuring that we held on to our family histories and literacies. She would icily remind those around her that she had attended community college, ran the accounting wing of her husband's car business, sent all three of her daughters to college, and, yes, she had at one time cleaned houses for a living. She spoke her accented English with a passion and confidence that made those without a second language seem less fortunate, less worldly, and less educated.

But I've also seen cracks in that armor of confidence, cracks that I often witness in younger multilingual/ELL students as they hit new strides in academic success, only to have moments when that success unravels and doubts about language return. As my mother aged into her seventies, I watched her doubts about her command of English return, especially in hospital settings, where she is often convinced that she doesn't understand, not because of the level of medical jargon being used but because, as she says now, "It's my English; it's not that good." When our multilingual students hit roadblocks in school, and even beyond school, similar moments of doubt emerge. Our goal as English teachers is to help them establish a sense of confidence and a command of language, particularly in their writing and self-expression, that remains long after they leave our classrooms and schools.

What's at Stake?

Mary Bucholtz and colleagues (2014) have noted that the work we do with multilingual students is not just about reading or writing; there is a vein of social justice threading through this work. Providing entryways into literacy for the millions of second language students in US secondary schools is not simply a matter of test scores, literacy, or even graduation rates. For many multilingual and ELL students trying to open the doors to education and more learning opportunities, the judgment about these students' trajectories happens on the written page. I've taught in middle schools and high schools where proficiency tests in writing determined whether or not a student could enter a mainstream ELA class. I've sat at conference tables with fellow teachers and guidance counselors, examining test scores and ELL students' writing portfolios in order to decide "appropriate" placement in tracking systems that rarely allowed students to move to upper-level classes. I've watched high school juniors craft and second-guess college admissions essays, trying to game the system, to understand what kind of narrative would appeal to an admissions board. I've seen ELL students fill out scholarship applications to enter programs like Upward Bound, trying to decide if they should reveal a parent's architectural degree from the Dominican Republic, or if revealing too much might mean they no longer qualify as first-generation college students. I've sat with first-year multilingual college students as they shared concerns about citation, error, and failing to make the grade in college composition, grades that would determine whether their scholarships would be available for another semester.

More and more, these kinds of experiences, coupled with reports from the fields of education, second language writing, and TESOL, convince me that the work we do as teachers of writing is not simply about transmitting a set of skills. Teaching writing well, particularly to those students on the margins of our schools and communities, is very much a social justice issue.

Social Justice on the Macro and Micro Levels in Our Teaching

> Politics with a capital *P* is the big stuff, the worldly concerns. . . . It is about governments and world trade agreements and the United Nations peacekeeping forces; it is about ethnic or religious genocide and world tribunals; it is about apartheid and global capitalism, money laundering, and linguistic imperialism. Politics with a "little *p*" connect to the minute-to-minute choices and decisions that make us who we are. . . . It is about desire and fear; how we construct them and how they construct us. It is about politics of identity and place; it is about small triumphs and defeats; it is about winners and losers, haves and have nots. . . . It is about how we treat other people day by day.
>
> —Hilary Janks (2010, p. 188)

I open this section with a wonderful quote from South African literacy researcher Hilary Janks, who speaks beautifully about what she sees as the ways we can begin to transform our teaching and the lives of our students. In her work, she notes the sometimes overwhelming aspects of big *P* Politics, which challenge some of the larger issues in our nations and our educational policies. But she also points to the little *p* politics that are much more connected to our daily choices, minute-to-minute decisions, and the small victories we can achieve with our students and in our classrooms. When I talk about working with ELL/multilingual writers as a social justice issue, I often hear from teachers overwhelmed by the larger justice issues (poverty, access, immigration, etc.) and educational policy issues (e.g., standards, assessments). As teachers we live in a world with many concerns and issues that we see our students, multilingual and monolingual, face daily. We are confronted with long-standing debates on education, standards, and classroom practices. We are often asked to defend our professional practices and are at times undermined in our efforts by powers that go far beyond our classroom walls. So when we consider social justice issues, I believe teachers, like Janks, often think of the capital letters: Social Justice in education. And the tasks and problems that face us and our students are both daunting and overwhelming.

The debates in these areas can often make teachers feel powerless, like ping-pong balls being tossed from one political agenda to the next. It's hard to believe that you can empower your students when you feel disempowered yourself.

So what can we do to try to feel less powerless? I suggest that one way to feel less powerless is to *transform our teaching*. The ways we teach writing, the methods we employ, and our resolve to help students feel empowered through their writing can help them articulate and achieve some measure of justice. By teaching in ways that are more inclusive and effective for the growing number of multilingual students in our schools, we can help make change.

Some changes, of course, come easier than others. In my talks with teachers and administrators, for example, I often encounter agreement when I discuss the strengths that linguistically and culturally diverse student bring to classrooms and schools. There is great empathy and interest in the stories of young immigrants, refugees, and bilinguals. The students know this too. The narrative that so many of them can and do weave about their multilingual, transnational experiences are often praised and held up as powerful examples of voice, fortitude, and storytelling at its best. Many teachers conscientiously stock classroom libraries with books showcasing diverse, multicultural characters and settings, and many teachers push to bring a diversity of authors from varying backgrounds, experiences, and countries into their reading lists. The content of the twenty-first-century ELA classroom demonstrates a commitment to multiculturalism in the curriculum, and these efforts reflect a broader commitment to social justice and diversity at the macro level.

At the same time, however, we need to be careful of becoming "multicultural tourists," who value and celebrate our students' accents, experiences, and cultures in the spaces beyond the daily curriculum, but don't question why those strengths are not valued in our assessments or in how we attend to writing instruction. I worry that there is a tendency to value and adopt the aspects of multiculturalism and culturally responsive teaching that are easiest—new books, new posters, multicultural days in our schools, listening to the stories of our students, learning about new holidays and language practices, etc. But it can be much harder to adopt new strategies and teaching practices. It can be much harder to take what we learn from our students and let that knowledge have a real impact on what and how we teach. Despite commitment to diverse content and genuine interest in the experiences of our students, there is often less commitment to adapting teaching strategies and lesson delivery in order to the meet the needs of these diverse students as readers and writers. To create opportunities for success with our ELL writers, we need to be ready to take on new teaching methods.

Day-to-Day Teaching as an Act of Advocacy

> Working with the politics of the local enables us in a different kind of transformative design.
>
> —Hilary Janks (2010, p. 188)

Adapting and changing our teaching methods, our lesson delivery, and our expectations so that they reflect a higher level of inclusivity is tricky. Issues of standards, standard English, and "accented" English make many teachers pause. Teachers worry about fairness and watering down the curriculum. But the shift to more inclusive writing instruction can also be viewed through the lens of social justice at the micro level: the small *social justice* as opposed to the large *Social Justice*. Quite simply, our most day-to-day tasks as writing teachers—lesson design, assignment design, responding to student writers, developing rubrics, and so on—can be framed in a social justice perspective. Writing instruction that is responsive to ELL/multilingual writers and that draws on best practices from TESOL can open up more opportunities for rich writing curricula, richer writing experiences, and greater progress for adolescent ELL writers. A move to new teaching practices is an important vehicle for social justice in our work with ELL students because taking up these approaches and techniques reveals a commitment to promoting ELL/multilingual student success and equal opportunity. Miller and Sylayeva, second language acquisition specialists, note that "a key tenant of social justice in education is to promote equal opportunities for all students in receiving a quality education while respecting the civil rights and cultural diversity of each individual" (2013, p. 13).

Getting Started

> If you have built castles in the air, your work need not be lost; that is where they should be. Now put the foundations under them.
> —Henry David Thoreau, *Walden*

If transforming our teaching is all about risk-taking and realizing the need for change, then reading this book is the first step toward transformation and rebuilding. Here you can imagine and begin to implement the changes you would like to see in your inclusive and responsive writing instruction and classroom practices. Consider some of the ideas presented in Chapters 3, 4, 5, and 6. What are some things you'd like to try? What small ideas would you like to incorporate into your daily teaching practices? How might you reframe your "beginning of the school year" assignments and activities in order to learn more about your students' literacies? What terms and ideas would you like to share with your students? What teaching strategies and methods would you like to try out with your student writers?

Consider new classroom procedures and habits that you'd like to incorporate in order to help the multilingual/ELL students in your class feel not only more welcome, but also like they can be "real writers" in your classroom. How might you adjust your assignments? How might your assignments include rhetorical fingerholds? How might you adjust timelines or implement new response procedures and feedback cycles into your work with ELLs?

The goal is to dream and make a list of the teaching strategies and changes you'd ideally like to bring to your classroom. Getting started is all about building up a new perspective for your course and classroom that sees multilingual students as part of your core audience.

Trying It Out

Here is where you begin to take out the new tools in your toolbox and try them out with students. Using new tools and strategies can be invigorating and full of "aha" moments for both teachers and students. But it can also be a time when some things don't work out as planned. The ideal lesson falls short. A deconstruction activity is met with blank stares and silence. Things don't go the way you dreamed they would. So now you tweak your plan. Reread, rewrite, and reflect. Troubleshoot and try again. When things fall short during this stage, you will go backwards. Jumping into culturally responsive teaching isn't going to happen without setbacks. And working with adolescents, who are grappling with their own conflicts, identities, and social concerns, is also part of this equation. Keep pushing forward, remembering that these students' literacy development is happening alongside their adolescence and their forays into identity development. When you encounter setbacks, seeking out others can be helpful. Talk to the ELL teacher down the hall; create an assignment that helps students teach you about their communities, their local heroes, and their aspirations. Invite members of these multilingual communities to your classroom to talk about reading and writing. Expect some setbacks, but also keep searching for and creating opportunities for small victories—for you and for your student writers.

Transforming our teaching is a dynamic, ever-changing process. New curricula get handed down, a new class ends up on your schedule, new students come to your school from another language group. Learning to work effectively with ELL/ multilingual writers is about developing a depth of knowledge about acquisition and writing in a second language, while at the same time being open and flexible to the new writers and the experiences they bring with them. In many ways, teaching with a social justice goal means that you begin to see working with ELL/multilingual writers as an integrated part of your teaching life.

Transforming the Lives of Our Students throughout Our Schools

A snapshot: Bruno, a sophomore from Ecuador, has been receiving ELL services for three years. He sits in the corner of the classroom, baseball cap pulled down, earbuds in his ears, wearing a T-shirt that he knows offends his teacher. He checks in and out of the teacher's lesson, looking up occasionally, and then slouching backwards, adjusting his phone. At one point, he jumps into the teacher-led workshop on nouns and plurals, offering up the difference between *man* and *men*. For a moment, I catch a glimmer of interest and a willingness to demonstrate something he knows; it strikes me that despite his slouching and earbuds, Bruno is still paying attention. He knows more than he lets on. But then just as quickly, he tunes out again, tapping at the screen of his smartphone, muttering, "I'm out. Because I had everything before," as the teacher announces that she will collect and grade last night's assignment. His notebook is empty.

Bruno's teacher is frustrated. He knows how to push her buttons, and she doesn't understand why he doesn't do his work. The sense of hopelessness on both sides is palpable.

After school that day, I see Bruno return to the same classroom but with a different teacher. The class is engaged in an afternoon extracurricular activity, and he's surrounded by other students; many of them are multilingual, some are not. All of them are from the school Spirit club, and some are also part of the ELL program. Bruno has turned his T-shirt inside out and the earbuds are no longer in his ears. He is working alongside his peers, talking about music, sharing a joke, and teaching Spanish words to the girl on his right. The group is working on posters for the sophomore class Spirit day. Bruno is helping the teacher, flirting with a girl politely, and looking for a ruler to make sure his lines and letters are straight. He's engaged and paying attention to details in the work before him. He wants to be sure his poster is the best, asking the teacher about the spelling of a word and checking with his peers about a potential slogan for the upcoming event. Here's the interesting thing: Bruno is still at school, an hour after the last bell has rung and the last bus has left. He's still here.

I share these moments from Bruno's day because we as teachers need to be open to seeing how our multilingual/ELL students might flourish in settings outside our classrooms. This is true for disengaged students like Bruno, but also for more engaged students, who are often just waiting for an invitation from a teacher to become part of some other aspect of their schools. As I've mentioned earlier, many ELL/multilingual students feel anonymous in their schools and particularly in their ELA classrooms. They often feel that certain activities—particularly those that link to writing—are off limits and really intended only for monolingual English speakers. We need to change that perception.

Many of us are committed to the lives of our students and our schools beyond the typical fifty-minute class time. We bring our passions into our school lives and impact our students in ways that often go beyond the daily curriculum. As a teacher committed to your students, you are probably involved with a number of other academic and extracurricular activities within your school. Some of you are working actively with drama clubs, literary magazines, school newspapers, outreach programs, school-to-work programs (that incorporate professional writing such as résumés and interviewing skills), book clubs, honor societies, talent shows, senior projects, sport teams, and much more. Others teach classes on creative writing or journalism as electives. Many of us are involved with extracurricular activities that intricately entwine with aspects of literacy, creativity, and writing. These are all additional places where we can begin to think about inclusivity and opportunities for our ELL/multilingual students. Teachers, administrators, and teacher educators can and should establish a supportive and responsive writing culture that fosters a broader, more inclusive writing community for teachers and all students within a school.

To that end, I want to explore three areas where we might expand our reach with ELL/multilingual writers and create more multilingual and inclusive opportunities for these writers in the "extracurriculum": creative writing, journalism, and drama.

Creative Writing

> Creative writing remains the language of the heart.
> —Yan Zhao (2015, p. 17)

In literature we have many examples of multilingual writers: poets, novelists, memoirists, romance writers, activists, playwrights. In many schools, these creative outlets are not offered to ELL/multilingual writers, and if they are offered, these young writers are often hesitant to join in. Given their often complicated relationship with writing, many ELL/multilingual writers need enthusiastic and explicit invitations from mentors and teachers to convince them that their voices and creativity are valued. This reluctance to engage with creative writing is also evident in the research on teaching the works of multilingual writers, research that focuses almost exclusively on academic writing, academic genres (argument, analysis, informational texts), and academic language (Zhao, 2015). A number of myths about these writers, and writing more generally, are embedded in this academic-only emphasis. One myth is that ELL writers aren't ready for creative writing. A second is that they don't have the time; there is so much these particular writers need to learn about academic English writing that needs to take precedence. A third related myth is that creative writing is not an academic priority; it's an "extra," something students can pursue on their own. All of these myths are reinforced by the fact that creative writing doesn't have a strong presence in the national standards movement.

But incorporating more creative writing opportunities into the school lives of ELL/multilingual writers needs to be a priority. Creative writing offers these youth an outlet for exploring new identities and experiences—to take on roles as narrators, to be original and creative, to become storytellers and poets, to relish the world of fiction, and to participate in the creativity that comes from wordplay and poetry. Creative writing, particularly when it's supported by teachers and schools, fosters unique ways for adolescent multilingual students to develop originality and offers occasions for choice and discovery. When multilingual writers are invited to pursue creativity in their writing, they are rewarded for curiosity and exploration, they are encouraged to take more risks with the written word, and they are filled with more motivation, particularly internal motivation, to pursue their words and voices.

Our students often view creative writing as something reserved only for the famous multilingual authors we have students read and share in our classrooms. Our multilingual students need to have more opportunities to see themselves as the writers of these kinds of stories. As writing researcher Yan Zhao has explained in her study of student writers and creative writing,

> L2 creative writing is no longer exclusive to the geniuses and talented; it becomes a socialization practice that flourishes in various sites outside the classroom, e.g. virtual spaces. Doing creative writing in one's L2 provides a medium for the performance of certain personas which could surpass the roles for L2 individuals as language learners, student, or just writers. (2015, p. 17)

Creative writing offers adolescent multilingual writers a place to experiment with language, voice, and story. It also becomes a place to incorporate various aspects of their identities, home communities, traditions, conflicts, and even home languages. Through creative writing, "bilingualism becomes a form of art beautifully played out in literary work" (p. 17).

These days, creative writing probably resides mainly in electives and the extracurriculum. Certainly the standards and testing movements have limited the kinds of writing that get taught in our classrooms and encouraged a focus on academic writing. However, we also know that creative writing still exists in our schools—in poetry units, in creative writing electives, in poetry and slam poetry clubs and contests, in fan fiction clubs, and in school literary ezines. As teachers of linguistically diverse students, we can make these kinds of opportunities more visible and more welcoming to these students in our schools. We need to do more to extend invitations, and we need to do more to encourage participation; ELA teachers can be agents of change. Consider how ELA teachers might create initiatives, activities, and venues that could embrace, celebrate, and publish the bilingual narratives, poems, and other texts created by these young writers in our schools. Examples of these kinds of publications are gaining prominence in many colleges, and similar initiatives are possible in middle and high schools. Here are a couple:

- *MotherTongue: A Multilingual Literary Journal* from the University of Massachusetts-Amherst—www.umass.edu/complit/mothertongue-journal
- *Toyon Literary Magazine* from Humboldt State University— www.toyonliterarymagazine.org/
- *Vagabond: Multilingual Journal*—http://vagabond.berkeley.edu/

Drama/Playwriting Classes

Along similar lines, teachers can encourage ELL/multilingual students to partici-pate in drama, film studies, and playwriting. These are wonderful creative spaces for students to explore their voices and tell their stories. Drama and screenwriting encourage students to practice writing, reading, and oral speech for real audiences. In Colorado, Greeley West High School provides an excellent model in the Gree-ley El Teatro program. Greeley El Teatro is a multilingual drama club. Students in the club write the shows themselves based on personal and familial experiences. The program started with shows that included both Spanish and English perfor-mances. In a recent production, the students' show was performed with twelve different languages, reflecting the diversity of languages in the school.

Even in those schools with fewer languages spoken or few ELL/multilin-gual students, teachers can think about how drama classes and even auditions can be made more open to students who aren't native English speakers. How can we increase the participation, presence, and creativity of these students in our schools? What kinds of invitations can we offer to encourage students to see themselves as part of this rich extracurricular fabric? What kinds of new activities or initiatives might make drama, film, and screenwriting more accessible and inclusive for our multilingual students? How might we help them see these activities and their inter-actions with peers in these groups not as a risk, but as a fun, inventive opportunity?

Community and Activist Writing Classes

Another avenue that is often underexplored for ELL/multilingual writers is re-search-based writing on communities and community issues. As standards like the CCSS push for students to write informational texts and engage in research-based writing, there are ways in which teachers can introduce genres in these categories that make the writing more engaging and meaningful for their ELL/multilingual students. For one, teachers can encourage students to focus on compelling issues that are affecting their families and their communities. Such writing assignments and projects promote civic engagement and encourage students to develop field-based and library-based research skills. One resource that may be particularly useful for ELA teachers trying to incorporate field-based research into their writing lessons is *Fieldworking: Reading and Writing Research* by Bonnie Sunstein and Elizabeth Chiseri-Strater (2012).

Community-based writing projects can also incorporate the use of digital historical archives. In one example of this kind of unit, Franquiz and Salinas (2011) encouraged newcomer multilingual students to examine historical archives of US social movements in various eras. Students then researched social issues in their own era that they had some knowledge about. Drawing on these documents and models, students then wrote persuasive and informational texts to government officials, community organizations, and other stakeholders about their findings and recommendations. Some students wrote persuasive and factual letters to President Obama and their congressional representatives in defense of the DREAM Act. As Franquiz and Salinas noted, "They crafted stances that were identity texts reflecting their own realities. Their writing sought support for themselves and their communities" (p. 208).

In addition to digital archives, teachers can share with students model texts from activist authors so they can see how such writers wrote passionately and factually about a number of historical eras and social issues. Potential authors might include Ida B. Wells, writing about race and violence in the South during the 1890s; Jonathan Kozol, writing about schools and childhood poverty in the United States; or Malala Yousafzai writing about female education in Pakistan, among others.

Journalism Classes

Journalism is another activity in which multilingual writers may find more opportunities to establish their voices. Most secondary schools have school newspapers and sometimes even a journalism course, but often multilingual students aren't recruited to join as reporters or take these courses. In fact, in one school where I worked, the school newspaper and their student reporters often reported on the ELL program, new student refugees, or some aspect of multilingualism in the community, but the student reporters were never multilingual themselves and most had limited contact with the ELL program and the students. In other words, ELL/multilingual students were viewed and written about but never asked to hold the pen and the voice recorder—never asked to be the reporters.

Teachers who serve as advisors for newspapers and yearbooks should consider how they can create more opportunities and invitations for the multilingual writers in their schools. What can multilingual students bring to the journalism class or newspaper? How can school publications highlight multilingualism as an asset? How can school publications be more accessible to a wider range of student readers? Here are some ideas that may help answer those questions:

- Publish sections of the school newspaper in multiple languages.

- Ask a multilingual student to serve as a columnist or reviewer. Consider how the column or review might be published in English and the author's first language.

- Ask a multilingual student to serve as a sports reporter and encourage him or her to pursue stories about student athletes from a variety of culture and language backgrounds.

- For students who are interested in reporting but nervous about participating, consider pairing up students into reporting teams. Help multilingual students see and draw on their strengths—as interviewers, as observers, and as story finders. Provide support and encouragement throughout the process.

- Publish interviews with multilingual leaders from communities, neighborhoods, government, business, etc.

- Share examples of student newspapers that encourage a multilingual perspective. One great example is *The Bronx Journal,* a student newspaper from CUNY's Lehman College produced by students in its Multilingual Journalism program. The newspaper produces supplements in at least six languages: http://bronxjournal.com/

Ideally, multilingual writers asked to write for their newspapers and taking part in journalism courses should also be groomed to take on leadership roles. Often, ELL students involved with these kinds of activities report that only monolingual English students are picked to be editors, and sometimes multilinguals shy away from these opportunities, influenced in part by a sense that their English isn't "good enough." But invitations from fellow students and teachers can empower multilingual students to feel that their voices and talents as reporters, writers, and editors are valuable to the staff and the school.

From Cycles of Inopportunity to Cycles of Opportunity

In the early pages of this book, I noted that so much of what ELL and multilingual writers encounter in our secondary schools is problematic. There are so many places and situations in which they encounter obstacles, discouragement, assignments, and even instruction that feed into what Kerry Enright and I have termed *cycles of inopportunity* (Ortmeier-Hooper & Enright, 2011). These cycles of inopportunity foster a self-belief among many of these students that they are not writers.

But we can change this narrative. We can nurture a more positive belief in these young multilingual writers and their texts. In the classroom and beyond the classroom, we can transform cycles of inopportunity into cycles of opportunity. We can establish classrooms and schools that offer these students a way to see their languages, experiences, and understandings of print and communication as assets and strengths. We can begin to build more inclusive writing classrooms that strengthen their skills, encourage their voices, and encourage the development of strategies that aid them in seeing that their teachers recognize them as owners of language and real writers. We can create curriculum and school structures that challenge monolingualism as the norm and that recognize the power of multilingualism and transnational knowledge in the twenty-first century. We can approach our teaching in ways that recognize these student writers as our own, integrated and essential to our classroom communities. We can applaud their victories and look for places where they can build on those successes. We can invite more of these students into upper-level academic tracks and then create curricula and initiatives that support them in these tracks. We can ask critical questions about how assessments are constructed, how multilingual writers are considered, and how these students' literacy strengths are valued. We can encourage our multilingual students to see that we value their voices and that they do indeed have something to write and say—and that we are listening.

Notes

1. A pseudonym.

2. In the first chapter, I introduced you to Mrs. Keller, an English and ELL teacher at an urban high school who works predominantly with high numbers of linguistically diverse writers, ages fourteen to eighteen. Throughout the following chapters, I will share examples from Mrs. Keller's classroom and others in order to illustrate how teachers can design inclusive assignments and develop responsive teaching strategies for their multilingual students.

3. Many of the students discussed in this book are adolescents who have literacy in their first languages. But I also want to acknowledge that there are many students, particularly new immigrants and refugees, who enter our schools with limited literacy and schooling experiences. This is particularly true of students whose education has been disrupted by poverty, malnutrition, war, trauma, or political unrest. These major gaps in education can impact students' levels of participation, as well as their other language learning skills. Even newcomers with high levels of literacy in their first language or experience in English can experience a "silent period" as they adjust to a new teacher or new school. Research studies on low educated second language and literacy acquisition (LESLLA), such as Bigelow and Vinogradov (2011) and Vinogradov (2012), offer teachers insights into best practices for their work with students who need help with emergent oral language and reading skills. ESL teachers in your building can be an important resource in helping ELA teachers identify which students may be LESLLA students and which students may have stronger language skills but feel shy or intimidated in the mainstream classroom.

Annotated Bibliography

The research on multilingual writers in US secondary schools has been somewhat limited over the past twenty years. But recently we have seen the emergence of uniquely skilled, invested teachers and researchers studying the writing and progress of adolescent multilingual students, informed by the rich traditions of second language writing, composition, bilingual education, and TESOL. There are growing numbers of studies dedicated to the specific concerns, challenges, and successes of these young writers and their teachers. Journals such as the *Journal of Second Language Writing* and the *Journal of Adolescent & Adult Literacy* include excellent publications from leaders in this area. In addition, the following short list of recommended resources includes useful books, along with "borrowings" from other areas of writing studies and second language acquisition. Some of these resources provide insights into the nature of writing and writer development; others point to specific aspects of teaching or an interesting question that offers up new possibilities for writing teachers. Each of them offers a place to begin, to learn, and to discover.

Brisk, María Estela
Engaging Students in Academic Literacies: Genre-Based Pedagogy for K–5 Classrooms.
New York: Routledge, 2015.

Brisk's extensive and thorough research on the use of systemic functional linguistics in elementary school classrooms provides a wealth of information for teachers interested in expanding their knowledge of SFL and deepening their use of the SFL method in the classroom. She provides discussions, additional lessons, and activities for building students' understanding of syntax and linguistic structures within a range of genres that will be useful to secondary school ELA and ELL teachers.

Bruce, Shanti, and Ben Rafoth, eds.
ESL Writers: A Guide for Writing Center Tutors.
Portsmouth, NH: Boynton/Cook, 2004.

Though originally designed for university writing center tutors, this book is a wonderful resource for classroom teachers in grades 7–12. In particular, the book includes excellent chapters on reading ELL student work and conferencing.

Conference on College Composition and Communication
CCCC Position Statement on Second Language Writing and Writers.
CCCC/National Council of Teachers of English, 2001, revised 2009, reaffirmed November 2014.

www.ncte.org/cccc/resources/positions/secondlangwriting

In 2001 the Conference on College Composition and Communication issued its first *Statement on Second Language Writing and Writers.* The 2009 revision of this policy document provides up-to-date information on best practices, multilingual students, writing across the curriculum, teaching training, class sizes, and more. It's an excellent advocacy tool for teachers who are concerned about the college-readiness of ELL/multilingual writers and who would like information on what are considered best institutional practices at the college level. It also includes an extensive bibliography of sources for those interested in learning more.

de Oliveira, Luciana C., Marshall Klassen, and Michael Maune, eds.
The Common Core State Standards in English Language Arts: For English Language Learners, Grades 6–12.
Alexandria, VA: TESOL Press, 2015

This collection of essays, published by TESOL, provides ELL and ELA teachers with insights into how to adapt the ELA Common Core State Standards for their work with multilingual students. It strives to help teachers set ambitious goals for students and provides ideas for how to engage students, increase their content knowledge, and strengthen their academic English across a range of reading and writing tasks.

de Oliveira, Luciana C., and Tony Silva, eds.
L2 Writing in Secondary Classrooms: Student Experiences, Academic Issues, and Teacher Education.
New York: Routledge, 2013.

This collection of empirical essays by scholars in the fields of second language writing, English education, and TESOL provides an insightful look at the experiences of teachers and multilingual/ELL students in US schools. The research-driven chapters consider ELL/multilingual writing in terms of broader educational policy, tracking and writing connections, student identity, and innovations in teacher education programs. Chapters look specifically at the impact of the Common Core State Standards, large-scale assessment practices, academic tracking, refugees, and student identity.

Ferris, Dana, and John Hedgcock
Teaching L2 Composition: Purpose, Process, and Practice. 3rd ed.
New York: Routledge, 2014.

This landmark book, now in its third edition, is a wealth of information for those new to working with multilingual writers at the college and secondary levels. Ferris and Hedgcock provide a comprehensive examination of the research on multilingual literacy practices, error correc-

tion, and L2 literacy development. The book also includes information on developing syllabi, choosing appropriate textbooks for students, grading, and assignments.

Ruecker, Todd
Transiciones: Pathways of Latinas and Latinos Writing in High School and College.
Logan: Utah State University Press, 2015.

Ruecker's monograph is a fascinating read that examines the pathways and stories of Latino/a high school students as they try to transition into college. The portraits and ethnographic research provide an intimate look into how sponsors, school success, tracking, and academic and personal disruptions help and hinder these students aspiring to attain their college degrees.

I also recommend the following website and film for those hoping to share multilingual/ELL writers' stories and experiences with colleagues and administrators:

•   The National Commission on Writing
    Words Have No Borders: Student Voices on Immigration, Language and Culture
    College Board, 2009.

    www.nwp.org/cs/public/download/nwp_file/12496/Words_Have_No_Borders.pdf?x-r=pcfile_d

•   Robertson, Wayne, dir.
    Writing across Borders.
    Corvallis: Oregon State University, Center for Writing and Learning, 2005.

    Segments of the film are available for viewing at www.youtube.com/watch?v=quI0vq9VF-c

References

Applebee, A., & Langer, J. (2011). *The national study of writing instruction: Methods and procedures.* [CELA Report]. Albany: Center on English Learning & Achievement, University of Albany. Retrieved from http://www.albany.edu/cela/reports/NSWI_2011_methods_procedures.pdf

Bigelow, M., & Vinogradov, P. (2011). Teaching adult second language learners who are emergent readers. *Annual Review of Applied Linguistics, 31,* 120–36.

Bomer, R. (2005). Meet our new students: English language learners in English language arts classrooms. *The Council Chronicle, 15*(2), 16.

Brandt, D. (2001). *Literacy in American lives.* New York: Cambridge University Press.

Brisk, M. E. (2015). *Engaging students in academic literacies: Genre-based pedagogy for K–5 classrooms.* New York: Routledge.

Bucholtz, M., Lopez, A., Mojarro, A., Skapoulli, E., VanderStouwe, C., & Warner-García, S. (2014). Sociolinguistic justice in the schools: Student researchers as linguistic experts. *Language and Linguistics Compass, 8*(4), 144–57. doi:10.1111/lnc3.12070

Canagarajah, A. S. (2013). *Translingual practice: Global Englishes and cosmopolitan relations.* Abingdon, UK, and New York: Routledge.

Chiang, Y-S. D., & Schmida, M. (2006). Language identity and language ownership: Linguistic conflicts of first-year university writing students. In P. K. Matsuda, M. Cox, J. Jordan, & C. Ortmeier-Hooper (Eds.), *Second-language writing in the composition classroom: A critical sourcebook* (pp. 95–108). New York: Bedford/St. Martin's Press.

Christie, F., & Derewianka, B. (2008). *School discourse: Learning to write across the years of schooling.* London: Continuum.

Common Core State Standards Initiative. (2010). *Common core state standards for English language arts and literacy in history/social studies, science, and technical subjects.* Retrieved from http://www.core standards.org/wp-content/uploads/ELA_Standards1.pdf

Conference on College Composition and Communication (CCCC). (2001). *CCCC statement on second language writing and writers.* NCTE/CCCC.

Conference on College Composition and Communication (CCCC). (2009). *CCCC statement on second language writing and writers.* NCTE/CCCC. Retrieved from http://www.ncte.org/cccc/resources/positions/secondlangwriting

Connor, U. (1996). *Contrastive rhetoric: Cross-cultural aspects of second-language writing.* Cambridge, UK: Cambridge University Press.

Connor, U. (2011). *Intercultural rhetoric in the writing classroom.* Ann Arbor: University of Michigan Press.

Crusan, D. (2010). *Assessment in the second language writing classroom.* Ann Arbor: University of Michigan Press.

Cox, M., & Zawacki, T.M. (Eds.). (2015). *WAC and second language writers: Research toward linguistically and culturally inclusive programs and practices.* Fort Collins, CO: WAC Clearinghouse; Anderson, SC: Parlor Press.

Cummins, J. (2005). Afterword. In K. Pahl, & J. Rowsell, *Literacy and education: Understanding the new literacy studies in the classroom* (pp. 140–52). London: Paul Chapman.

Cummins, J. (2006). Multiliteracies pedagogy and the role of identity texts. In K. Leithwood, P. McAdie, N. Bascia, & A. Rodrigue. (Eds.) *Teaching for deep understanding: What every educator should know* (pp. 85–93). Thousand Oaks, CA: Corwin Press.

Cummins, J., Bismilla, V., Chow, P., Cohen, S., Giampapa, F., Leoni, L., Sandhu, P., & Sastri, P. (2005). Affirming identity in multilingual classrooms. *Educational Leadership, 63*(1), 38–43.

Currie, P. (1998). Staying out of trouble: Apparent plagiarism and academic survival. *Journal of Second Language Writing, 7*(1), 1–18.

de Oliveira, L. C. (Ed.). (2013). *Teacher education for social justice: Perspectives and lessons learned.* Charlotte, NC: Information Age.

de Oliveira, L. C., & Iddings, J. (Eds.). (2014). *Genre pedagogy across the curriculum: Theory and application in U.S. classrooms and contexts.* Sheffield, UK: Equinox.

de Oliveira, L. C., Klassen, M., & Maune, M. (Eds.). (2015). *The Common Core State Standards in language arts, grades 6–12.* Alexandria, VA: TESOL Press.

Derewianka, B. (1990). *Exploring how texts work.* Rozelle, NSW: Primary English Teaching Association.

Derewianka, B., & Jones, P. (2013). *Teaching language in context.* South Melbourne, Vic., AU: Oxford University Press.

Didiot-Cook, H., Gauthier, V., & Scheirlinckx, K. (2000). Language needs in business, a survey of multinational companies. *LSE Research Online.* HEC Paris, Languages and Cultures Department working paper, 725. Inter-faculty Group for Languages Joint Study Project. Community of European Management Schools. Retrieved from http://eprints.lse.ac.uk/24729/1/Didiot-Cook_%20etal_Language-needs-in-business_2000.pdf

Echevarría, J., Vogt, ME., & Short, D. (2010). *Making content comprehensible for elementary English learners: The SIOP model.* Boston: Allyn and Bacon.

Enright, K. A. (2010). Academic literacies and adolescent learners: English for subject-matter secondary classrooms. *TESOL Quarterly, 44*(4), 804–10.

Enright, K. A. (2011). Language and literacy for a new mainstream. *American Educational Research Journal, 48*(1), 80–118.

Enright, K. A., & Gilliland, B. (2011). Multilingual writing in an age of accountability: From policy to practice in U.S. high school classrooms. *Journal of Second Language Writing, 20*(3), 182–95.

Ferris, D. R. (2002). *Treatment of error in second language student writing.* Ann Arbor: University of Michigan Press.

Ferris, D. R. (2003). *Response to student writing: Implications for second language students.* Mahwah, NJ: Lawrence Erlbaum.

Ferris, D. R. (2006). Does error feedback help student writers? New evidence on the short- and long-term effects of written error correction. In K. Hyland & F. Hyland (Eds.), *Feedback in second language writing: Contexts and issues* (pp. 81–102). New York: Cambridge University Press.

Ferris, D. R., & Hedgcock, J. S. (2005). *Teaching ESL composition: Purpose, process, and practice* (2nd ed.). Mahwah, NJ: Erlbaum.

Ferris, D. R, & Hedgcock, J. S. (2013). *Teaching L2 composition: Purpose, process, and practice* (3rd ed.). New York: Routledge.

Franquiz, M. E., & Salinas, C. S. (2011). Newcomers developing English literacy through historical thinking and digitized primary sources. *Journal of Second Language Writing, 20*(3), 196–210.

Fu, D. (1995). *My trouble is my English: Asian students and the American dream.* Portsmouth, NH: Boynton/Cook/Heinemann.

Fu, D. (2009). *Writing between languages: How English language learners make the transition to fluency, grades 4–12.* Portsmouth, NH: Heinemann.

García, O. (2012). Theorizing translanguaging for educators. In C. Celic & K. Seltzer (Eds.), *Translanguaging: A CUNY-NYSIEB guide for educators* (pp. 1–7). New York: CUNY-NYSIEB.

García, O., & Beardsmore, H. B. (2011). *Bilingual education in the 21st century: A global perspective.* Hoboken, NJ: John Wiley & Sons.

García, O., & Kleifgen, J. A. (2010). *Educating emergent bilinguals: Policies, programs, and practices for English language learners.* New York: Teachers College Press.

García, O., & Kleyn, T. (Eds.). (2016). Translanguaging with multilingual students: Learning from classroom moments. New York: Routledge.

García, O., & Wei, L. (2014). *Translanguaging: Language, bilingualism and education* (pp. 63–77). London: Palgrave Macmillan.

Geary, C. (1999). Missing. In J. Kitchen & M. P. Jones (Eds.), *In brief: Short takes on the personal* (pp. 134–35). New York: W. W. Norton.

Giampapa, F. (2010). Multiliteracies, pedagogy and identities: Teacher and student voices from a Toronto elementary school. *Canadian Journal of Education, 33*(2), 407–31.

Goldstein, L. M. (2005). *Teacher written commentary in second language writing classrooms*. Ann Arbor: University of Michigan Press.

Graff, G., & Birkenstein, C. (2010). *They say/I say: The moves that matter in academic writing* (2nd ed.). New York: Norton.

Halliday, M. A. K. (1985). *An introduction to functional grammar*. London: Arnold.

Hamp-Lyons, L., & Condon, W. (2000). *Assessing the portfolio: Principles for practice, theory, and research*. Cresskill, NJ: Hampton Press.

Hanson, J. (2013). Moving out of the monolingual comfort zone and into the multilingual world: An exercise for the writing classroom. In A. Suresh Canagarajah (Ed.), *Literacy as translingual practice: Between communities and classrooms* (pp. 207–14). New York: Routledge.

Harklau, L. (1994). ESL versus mainstream classes: Contrasting second language learning contexts. *TESOL Quarterly, 28*(2), 241–72.

Haynie, D. (2014, November 17). Number of international college students continues to climb. *US News & World Report*. Retrieved from https://www.usnews.com/education/best-colleges/articles/2014/11/17/number-of-international-college-students-continues-to-climb

Hinds, J. (1987). Reader versus writer responsibility: a new typology. In U. Connor & R. B. Kaplan (Eds.), *Writing across languages: Analysis of L2 text* (pp. 14X–152). Reading, MA: Addison-Wesley.

Hirvela, A. (2004). *Connecting reading and writing in second language writing instruction*. Ann Arbor: University of Michigan Press.

Hyland, K. (2003). *Second language writing*. New York: Cambridge University Press

Institute of International Education and Department of State Bureau of Educational and Cultural Affairs. (2014, November 17). 2014 Open Doors press briefing Washington DC. Retrieved from https://www.iie.org/en/Why-IIE/Events/2014-Open-Doors-Press-Briefing-Washington-DC

Janks, H. (2010). *Literacy and power*. New York: Routledge.

Johns, A. M. (1999). Opening our doors: Applying socioliterate approaches (SA) to language minority classrooms. In L. Harklau, K. M. Losey, & M. Siegal (Eds.), *Generation 1.5 meets college composition: Issues in the teaching of writing to U.S.-educated learners of ESL* (pp. 159–71). Mahwah, NJ: Erlbaum.

Johns, A. M. (2011). Opening our doors: Applying socioliterate approaches (SA) to language minority classrooms. In P. K. Matsuda, M. Cox, J. Jordan, & C. Ortmeier-Hooper (Eds.), *Second-language writing in the composition classroom: A critical sourcebook* (pp. 290–302). New York: Bedford/St. Martin's. (Reprinted from L. Harklau, K. M. Losey, & M. Siegal (Eds.). (1999). *Generation 1.5 meets college composition: Issues in the teaching of writing to US-educated learners of ESL*. Mahwah, NJ: Lawrence Erlbaum.)

Kanno, Y., & Kangas, S. E. N. (2014). "I'm not going to be, like, for the AP": English language learners' limited access to advanced college-preparatory courses in high school. *American Educational Research Journal, 51*(5), 848–78.

Kibler, A. (2011). "I write it in a way that people can read it": How teachers and adolescent L2 writers describe content area writing. *Journal of Second Language Writing, 20*(3), 211–26.

Kittle, P. (2008). *Write beside them: Risk, voice, and clarity in high school writing*. Portsmouth, NH: Heinemann.

Komunyakaa, Y. (1999). The deck. In J. Kitchen, & M. P. Jones (Eds.), *In brief: Short takes on the personal* (pp. 234–35). New York: W. W. Norton. Also available at https://www.ibiblio.org/ipa/poems/komunyakaa/deck.php

Kramer-Simpson, E. A. (2012). *Learning from feedback: How students read, interpret and use teacher written feedback in the composition classroom* (Doctoral Dissertation, University of New Hampshire). Available from ProQuest Dissertations and Theses database. (UMI No. 3533706)

Larsen, D. (2013). Focus on pre-service preparation for ESL writing instruction: Secondary teacher perspectives. In L. C. de Oliveira & T. Silva (Eds.), *L2 Writing in secondary classrooms: Student experiences, academic issues, and teacher education* (pp. 119–32). New York: Routledge.

Leki, I. (1992a). Building expertise through sequenced writing assignments. *TESOL Journal*, *1*(2), 19–23.

Leki, I. (1992b). *Understanding ESL writers: A guide for teachers*. Portsmouth, NH: Boynton/Cook.

Leki, I. & Carson, J. (1994). Students' perceptions of EAP writing instruction and writing needs across the disciplines. *TESOL Quarterly*, *28*(1), 81–101.

Li, X. (2005). Composing culture in a fragmented world: The issue of representation in cross-cultural research. In P. K. Matsuda & T. Silva (Eds.), *Second language writing research: Perspectives on the process of knowledge construction* (pp. 119–32). Mahwah, NJ: Lawrence Erlbaum.

Lipstein, R. L., & Renninger, K. A. (2007). "Putting things into words": The development of 12-15-year-old students' interest for writing. In S. Hidi, & P. Boscolo (Eds.), *Writing and motivation* (pp. 113–40). Amsterdam: Elsevier.

Liu, J., & Hansen, J. G. (2002). *Peer response in second language writing classrooms*. Ann Arbor: University of Michigan Press.

Matsuda, P. K. (1997). Contrastive rhetoric in context: A dynamic model of L2 writing. *Journal of Second Language Writing*, *6*(1), 45–60.

Matsuda, P. K. (2006). The myth of linguistic homogeneity in US college composition. *College English*, *68*(6), 637–51.

Matsuda, P. K., & Cox, M. (2011). Reading an ESL writer's text. *Studies in Self-Access Learning Journal*, *2*(1), 4–14.

Matsuda, P. K., & Hammill, M. J. (2014). Second language writing. In G. Tate, A. R. Taggart, K. Schick, & H. B. Hessler (Eds.), *A guide to composition pedagogie* (2nd ed., pp. 266–82). New York: Oxford University Press.

May, S. (Ed.). (2013). *The multilingual turn: Implications for SLA, TESOL and bilingual education*. New York: Routledge.

Miller, G., & Sylayeva, L. (2013). Socially just teaching through the eyes of Russian immigrants. In L. C. de Oliveira (Ed.), *Teacher education for social justice: Perspectives and lessons learned* (11–22). Charlotte, NC: Information Age.

Moll, L., Saez, R., & Dorwin, J. (2001). Exploring biliteracy: Two student case examples of writing as a social practice. *The Elementary School Journal*, *101*(4), 435–49.

Murray, D. M. (1995). *The craft of revision* (2nd ed.). Fort Worth, TX: Harcourt Brace.

National Center for Education Statistics (NCES). (2017). *English language learners in public schools*. Retrieved from https://nces.ed.gov/programs/coe/indicator_cgf.asp

National Commission on Writing. (2004). *Writing: A ticket to work . . . or a ticket out: A survey of business leaders*. The College Board. Retrieved from www.writingcommission.org/prod_downloads/writingcom/writing-ticket-to-work.pdf

National Council of Teachers of English (NCTE). (2007). *Globalization and English education*. [Archived report]. Retrieved from http://www.ncte.org/archive/cee/2007summit/globalization/1505.arch

Ortega, L. (2014). Ways forward for a bi/multilingual turn in SLA. In S. May (Ed.), *The multilingual turn: Implications for SLA, TESOL and bilingual education* (pp. 32–53). New York: Routledge.

Ortmeier-Hooper, C. (2008). "English may be my second language, but I'm not 'ESL.'" *College Composition and Communication*, *59*(3), 389–419.

Ortmeier-Hooper, C. (2013). *The ELL writer: Moving beyond basics in the secondary classroom*. New York: Teachers College Press.

Ortmeier-Hooper, C., & Enright, K. A. (2011). Mapping new territory: Toward an understanding of adolescent L2 writers and writing in U.S. contexts. *Journal of Second Language Writing*, *20*(3), 167–81.

Raimes, A. (1985). What unskilled ESL students do as they write: A classroom study of composing. *TESOL Quarterly*, *19*(2), 229–58.

Reid, J., & Kroll, B. (1995). Designing and assessing effective classroom assignments for NES and ESL students. *Journal of Second Language Writing*, *4*(1), 17–41.

Roberge, M., Siegal, M., & Harklau, L. (Eds.). (2009). *Generation 1.5 in college composition: Teaching ESL to U.S.-educated learners of ESL*. New York: Routledge.

Ruecker, T. (2015). *Transiciones: Pathways of Latinas and Latinos writing in high school and college.* Logan, UT: Utah State University Press.

Schleppegrell, Mary J. (2004). *The Language of Schooling: A functional linguistics perspective.* Mahwah, NJ: Lawrence Erlbaum.

Schleppegrell, M. J. & Go, A. (2007). Analyzing the writing of English learners: A functional approach. *Language Arts, 84*(6), 529–38.

Silva, T. (1993). Toward an understanding of the distinct nature of L2 writing: The ESL research and its implications. *TESOL Quarterly, 27*(4), 657–77.

Silva, T. (1997). On the ethical treatment of ESL writers. *TESOL Quarterly, 31*(2), 359–63.

Sunstein, B. S., & Chiseri-Strater, E. (2012). *Fieldworking: Reading and writing research* (4th ed.). Boston: Bedford/St. Martins.

United Nations Department of Economic and Social Affairs. (2005). *Summary of the report of the Global Commission on International Migration.* New York: Global Commission on International Migration (GCIM). Retrieved from http://www.un.org/esa/population/meetings/fourthcoord2005/P09_GCIM.pdf

US Department of Education. (2006, July 27). Building partnerships to help English language learners. [Info sheet on No Child Left Behind legislation]. Retrieved from http://www2.ed.gov/nclb/methods/english/lepfactsheet.pdf.

Valdés, G. (2003). *Expanding definitions of giftedness: The case of young interpreters from immigrant backgrounds.* Mahwah, NJ: Lawrence Erlbaum.

Villalva, K. A. [Enright]. (2006a). Hidden literacies and inquiry approaches of bilingual high school writers. *Written Communication, 23*(1), 91–129.

Villalva, K. A. [Enright]. (2006b). Reforming high school writing: Opportunities and constraints for generation 1.5 writers. In P. K. Matsuda, C. Ortmeier-Hooper, & X. You (Eds.), *The politics of second language writing: In search of the promised land* (pp. 30–56). West Lafayette, IN: Parlor Press.

Vinogradov, P. (2012). "You just get a deeper understanding of things by talking:" Study circles for teachers of ESL emergent readers. *Journal of Research and Practice for Adult Literacy, Secondary, and Basic Education, 1*(1), 30–43.

Weigle, S. C. (2002). *Assessing writing.* Cambridge, UK: Cambridge University Press.

Wight, S. (2015). *"Upward bound is college bound": Pre-college outreach programs' sponsorship of academic writing* (Doctoral dissertation). Retrieved from ProQuest Dissertations & Theses A&I. (1697922559)

Wight, S. (2017, May 8). Admitted or denied: Multilingual writers negotiate admissions essays. *Journal of Adolescent & Adult Literacy.* doi:10.1002/jaal.667

Wilson, M. (2006). *Rethinking rubrics in writing assessment.* Portsmouth, NH: Heinemann.

Wilson, M. (2007). Why I won't be using rubrics to respond to students' writing. *English Journal 96*(4), 62–66.

You, X. (2010). *Writing in the Devil's tongue: A history of English composition in China.* Carbondale, IL: Southern Illinois University Press.

Zawacki, T. M., Hajabbasi, E., Habib, A., Antram, A., & Das, A. (2007). *Valuing written accents: Non-native students talk about identity, academic writing, and meeting teachers' expectations.* Fairfax, VA: George Mason University Diversity Research Group and Offices of University Life, University Writing Center.

Zhao, Y. (2015). *Second language creative writers: Identities and writing processes.* Bristol, UK: Multilingual Matters.

Zhu, W. (2001). Interaction and feedback in mixed peer response groups. *Journal of Second Language Writing, 10*(4), 251–76.

Index

Author

Christina Ortmeier-Hooper is an associate professor and director of composition at the University of New Hampshire, where she teaches first-year writing, advanced composition, and teacher education courses, as well as graduate courses in teacher research, composition theory, and multilingual literacies and writing. As a former secondary school teacher, her interests continue to be anchored in working with teachers and multilingual adolescents as they navigate the expectations for writing, reading, and language in secondary schools and college. Ortmeier-Hooper is the author and editor of various books, including *Reinventing Identities in Second Language Writing* (2010), with Michelle Cox, Jay Jordan, and Gwen Gray Schwartz; *The ELL Writer: Moving beyond Basics in the Secondary Classroom* (2013); and *Linguistically Diverse Immigrant and Resident Writers: Transitions from High School to College* (2017), coedited with Todd Ruecker. She regularly speaks and works with teachers nationally on a range of writing and literacy initiatives.

This book was typeset in Janson Text and BotonBQ by
Barbara Frazier.

Typefaces used on the cover include American Typewriter,
Frutiger, and Formata.

The book was printed on 60-lb. White Recycled Offset paper
by Versa Press, Inc.